WITHD

'G SHIFT

ALSO BY MARC FREEDMAN

*Encore: Finding Work That
Matters in the Second Half of Life*

*Prime Time: How Baby Boomers Will
Revolutionize Retirement and Transform America*

*The Kindness of Strangers: Adult Mentors,
Urban Youth, and the New Voluntarism*

The
BIG
SHIFT

*Navigating the New Stage
Beyond Midlife*

MARC FREEDMAN

PUBLICAFFAIRS
New York

Copyright © 2011 by Marc Freedman
Published in the United States by PublicAffairs™, a member of the
Perseus Books Group.
Paperback edition first published in 2012 by PublicAffairs™.

PublicAffairs books are available at special discounts for bulk
purchases in the U.S. by corporations, institutions, and other
organizations. For more information, please contact the Special
Markets Department at the Perseus Books Group, 2300 Chestnut
Street, Suite 200, Philadelphia, PA 19103, call (800) 810-4145, ext.
5000, or e-mail special.markets@perseusbooks.com.

Library of Congress has catalogued the printed edition as follows:

Freedman, Marc.
    The big shift : navigating the new stage beyond midlife / Marc
Freedman. — 1st ed.
        p. cm.
    Includes bibliographical references and index.
    1. Middle-aged persons—Life skills guides. 2. Middle age—
Psychological aspects. 3. Old age—Planning. 4. Self-actualization
(Psychology) I. Title.
    HQ1059.4.F74 2011
    646.70084'4—dc22

                                        2010053183

ISBN 978-1-58648-785-0 (hardcover)
ISBN 978-1-61039-099-6 (paperback)
ISBN 978-1-58648-918-2 (e-book)

10 9 8 7 6 5 4 3 2

FOR LESLIE,
with love and appreciation

&

FOR GABRIEL, LEVI, AND MICAH,
our own little generativity revolution

We rarely come to anything like a masterly grip till the shadows begin to slant eastward, and for a season, which varies greatly with individuals, our powers increase as the shadows lengthen.

—G. STANLEY HALL,
Senescence: The Last Half of Life (1922)

CONTENTS

ONE

An AARP Discount— and Two Cribs

· ·

I turned fifty and decided to take a break. After twenty-five years of working, it seemed like a good idea. Honestly, I was feeling depleted. I still cared about my career and realized, amid a worsening economic climate, that I was lucky to have one. But that appreciation felt more lodged in my head than my heart.

One day, United Airlines sent me a card, along with some new luggage tags, offering congratulations on having flown 2 million miles. Quick arithmetic translated all those zeroes into the equivalent of flying from one side of the country to the other every single day—Sundays, holidays, birthdays, sick or well— for more than two years. Maybe the card from United should have offered condolences. It all added up to an abiding fatigue. And a question: Did I want to fly 2 million more miles over the next twenty-five years of my life?

Was I having a low-grade midlife crisis? I had no red sports car, reckless affair, or other obvious sign something was amiss. Instead, there seemed to be internal bleeding—a sense that the energy and optimism were ebbing out of me. My hope was that a three-month sabbatical would cure all that, bringing needed rest and clarity. After ten years of running the organization I'd founded, I thought I might be able to arrange some combination of vacation and leave. My board, perhaps a little worried about me as well, was happy to oblige.

I resolved to get away, far away. Soon I was looking at hotel reservations in Australia, contemplating time in Southeast Asia, marking off several months in the calendar. I purchased plane tickets, for myself, my wife, and our kids. Then the reality set in—the cost, the time away, living out of a suitcase for weeks on end. It all sounded eerily like one more business trip. A down payment on the road to 3 million miles? Do they give you the actual luggage when you hit that milestone?

I canceled the Australian hotels. I called the airlines to say forget it. They informed me that not taking my trip would cost $1,000 in penalties. I contemplated returning my luggage tags in protest. Soon, however, to my surprise, liberation was replacing disappointment. The lightness reminded me of research findings suggesting one of life's great joys was *not* taking a big vacation after the pleasures of anticipating one. Planning a trip, basking in the possibilities, experiencing the entire journey in one's mind—those were the fun parts. Lugging bags, dealing with surly employees, battling airport security, spending more money than budgeted, and eventually returning home exhausted and confronting a pile of mail and accumulated obligations—in other words, taking the actual vacation—were much less enjoyable. The perfect combination, at least according to this research, turns out to be planning fantastic adventures and then bailing out at the last minute.

Yet, research notwithstanding, I still wanted to get away and clear my head. My three-month sabbatical Down Under was downsized into a two-week car trip in a dented Prius up the Pacific Coast from San Francisco, where I live, to Oregon. After consulting the map and locating the midpoint for our journey, I got on the phone with the Homewood Suites in Medford, Oregon, to make reservations for our first stop en route to the Pacific Northwest. In the spirit of frugality—after all, I was already out a thousand bucks before our trip had even started—I asked about discounts. The AAA rate knocked off 20 percent. Great. Then it dawned on me. I was fifty years old, after all. I had shelled out for the AARP card when prompted. What about the "senior" discount? It was the lowest rate. Book it, I told the twentysomething clerk, and hung up the phone triumphant. I was already beginning to envision the new trip, when I remembered my wife's injunction about requesting cribs for our two boys, ages one and three, part of the reason we weren't checking in at the Sydney Marriott.

The same clerk answered again. Yes, I was the guy he'd just talked to, with the senior discount. I'd like to request two cribs in the room, I said. Yes, that's right, an AARP discount and two cribs. Was that the fraud alert beeping in the background? I know I heard something. I fully expected to be carded by the clerk upon check-in, perhaps flanked by local law enforcement.

HOMEWOOD BOUND

The Homewood Suites of Medford provided a memorable moment: Our one-year-old took his first steps on the hotel room's recently laid carpet, as we followed him around with the video camera. The stay was significant in another way as well. In that moment on the phone with the reservation clerk, a series of truths about my quiet crisis became evident.

The odd combination of discounts and requests—signs of what once indicated distinct parts of the life cycle separated by decades—made one thing abundantly clear and personal: The old map of life, which guided us for generations, was rapidly becoming an anachronism.

Until not long ago, the fifties and sixties meant retirement, grandparenthood, senior discounts, and early-bird specials. Possibly contemplating a retirement community free from school taxes and frequent visits by anyone under eighteen. Maybe even an end to working. My own father took the early-out package at fifty-seven, with 80 percent of his top salary guaranteed for life. Now twenty-three years into retirement, he has a decent shot at being retired for as long as he worked and earning more money for not working than he earned for getting up and going to the job each day. That won't be possible—or sustainable—for me.

By the time my dad was fifty, I had already graduated from college, and my sister was nearly done. By the time my third son—yes, we had another one since the trip—is through college, I will likely be closing in on my eightieth birthday, my father's age today. Like so many others, I delayed parenthood until my second marriage. It's a joy and I have no regrets, but I wonder how I'll wrestle with my kids without wrenching my back and how I'll pay college tuition in my seventies. I wonder what it will mean for my working life.

There's also a question of identity. What's the category for people like me? There are a growing number of us who can be classified as neither-nors. Neither young nor old. Neither retirees nor of traditional parenting age. Tired, perhaps, but neither ready to be retired nor able to afford it. The truth is, I will probably be working for another twenty-five years, the second half of my adult life.

What's more, this isn't just about me or my boomer colleagues. New research suggests that children the age of my kids, growing up in the developed world, can reasonably expect to see their one hundredth birthdays. The odds of doing so, by some estimates, exceed 50 percent. In other words, those of us hitting fifty today are simply the first generation to inhabit an emerging lifecourse, one that is in flux but will be a permanent change, not a passing aberration.

My Medford moment brought with it another juxtaposition. For me, the personal and professional were merging in a way I hadn't seen coming, even though it should have been excruciatingly easy to spot. In my thirties I started Civic Ventures, an organization focused on helping America make the most of the coming demographic revolution by enabling people to move into new jobs for the greater good after age fifty. We call these "encore careers," a kind of practical idealism at the intersection of continued income, deeper meaning, and social impact.

For some time, I'd been promoting all the benefits to be reaped by more individuals making the leap from the desire to find a new calling in the second half of adulthood to a life built around these aspirations. Burned out? Do something else, especially since you'll probably have to work for decades more. May as well find something you can look forward to doing when you get up all the many mornings to come. Not sure what you want to do next? Consider taking time off to experiment. The expense? It's worth it if you plan to work in your encore career for another ten, fifteen, twenty years. Facing economic downturn? Education, health, and public-sector work are the most recession-resistant sectors, full of jobs that might appeal to people looking for work that matters.

I had a lot of advice for others, all those folks presumably older than I was. Now the person looking back in the mirror not only qualifies for the AARP discount but also looks like he qualifies. (I did not get carded when I showed up at the check-in counter at the Homewood Suites.) What about taking my own advice? Not so easy while supporting a family of five, weighed down by a mortgage acquired at the height of the real estate boom. And then there's health insurance. For a whole set of practical reasons, I felt stuck. What wisdom did I have for myself?

Sure, I was at a natural transition point. Twenty-five years laboring in, essentially, the same vineyard. I had established some standing as an authority on finding meaning in the second half of life, particularly through career change. But here I was facing all the barriers to making a shift—psychological inertia, financial risk, the reality that my search for happiness was inextricably intertwined with the dreams and happiness of four other people (also known as my family . . . three of them still shy of kindergarten). I started resenting the easy advice dispensed by lifestyle magazines—and experts like me.

Then an additional element entered the mix. Several years ago a colleague noticed my hands shaking and suggested that I go see someone about it. I was convinced the tremors were the result of too much coffee, but after several others offered similar counsel, I made an appointment with a neurologist. She put me through a battery of tests, including an MRI of the brain. The test revealed nothing worrisome. The doctor diagnosed "benign essential tremors," with an emphasis on the *benign* over the *essential*—and a recommendation to cut back on the caffeine. I was instructed to check back in a couple of years. It took me three, but this time when the neurologist ran through her routine, which I assumed would be routine, the concern on her face was evident. She advised me to see someone who specialized in Parkinson's disease. Starting to panic, I asked her to level with me. I wouldn't hold her to it, but what was she really thinking? What were the chances I had Parkinson's? She told me they were fifty-fifty.

A week from the due date for our third child, I found myself rewriting the future in my head. A sense of dread began forming, aided by Internet searches revealing grim prospects, plus a very long wait to see a doctor. After three months, I was finally able to see Parkinson's specialists at the University of California at San Francisco, who examined me thoroughly, for hours. Their conclusion was that I didn't have the disease. An enormous weight lifted. Still, there was a residue, a new perspective, a sense of the finiteness of life and the precariousness of health. And, at the same time, the recognition that I'd likely be healthy for decades to come. Time had been compressed and had then expanded again. The question of how I was going to spend the next twenty-five years took on a new cast.

LOOKING BACK, LOOKING AHEAD

Of course, I knew that I was hardly alone in my unease. In logging those millions of miles, I'd heard the same refrain dozens of times from people I'd once considered "aging." But now, I was hearing it from my friends and colleagues, from my own mouth. We weren't old, but we were all navigating similar challenges, similar changes.

One friend first survived a bout with melanoma, and then a few years later his wife asked for a divorce just as the second of their two children headed off to college. He was left with a new sense of insecurity after the settlement. Marriage over, kids grown, house sold, savings depleted. "My life imploded," he told me. What's more, his commitment to his job as a lawyer was also wavering. He had been just about the only person I knew who loved being a lawyer. After surviving turns representing Hollywood clients, a final barking-dog case pitting one misanthropic neighbor against another ended his romance with private practice. Within months he moved from Los Angeles to Washington, D.C., to take a job as assistant general counsel at a federal agency, renting a modest apartment, taking a substantial pay cut, and starting over in a line of work that he hoped would provide not just a change of scenery but a new sense of purpose.

A few months earlier, I'd picked up the Sunday *New York Times* to read an article in the Business section about an acquaintance from college, whom I remembered as particularly driven and brilliant. She won a prestigious international fellowship in our second year. Soon after graduation, she landed a lucrative job on Wall Street, where she by all accounts prospered for decades. The *Times* article was her personal reflection on being laid off, stripped not only of her livelihood but also a major part of her identity. She was now in the throes of trying to make a transition, at last liberated by being tossed out of work that had lost its appeal. Yet she was still interviewing for banking jobs while trying to convince nonprofit organizations that her skills would translate to a new role. "I found myself struggling with one path that looked backward to what I knew and another that would go forward in an unfamiliar direction," she wrote.

I soon realized that one after another of my fiftysomething friends were themselves wrestling with a shift, feeling a growing pull not only toward a new phase of work but toward a different kind of life and a new set of priorities as well. Many likewise felt stymied by a variety of barriers. For every one who'd been visited by a health crisis, a divorce, a layoff, there seemed to be several more who were thinking that a new direction was needed. Yet we were all unsure of the path from what's past to what's next. We lacked a language even to talk about this change, which felt for many simultaneously self-indulgent and imperative. They were asking the same questions gnawing at me: How can I find rest and renewal? How do I make a change? How do I get started? How do I finance this transition? What if things don't work out? Will I be any good at something new? Can I take a big risk in my life when my situation is so intertwined with the well-being of others? How can I live a life that has greater significance, that leaves the world a better place? If I don't make that change now, will it be too late? I'd heard it all before, yet it all seemed new to me, so puzzling when at earlier points in my life, it had all seemed so simple.

This book grew out of a desire to make sense of what was happening in my own life, in the lives surrounding me, in the circumstances of many others at a similar juncture, especially in the context of economic pressures that were forcing more and more people to rethink assumptions about the future, about what's next and what matters most. My instinct was toward stories. What could the role models just ahead of us on this journey impart about their experiences, both the more uplifting moments and the times of despair? What lessons had they wrested from their encounters? Perhaps, most significantly, why is this transition so hard if so many people are feeling the same thing, at the same time, in sizable numbers?

I put on more miles, talking to hundreds of individuals in dozens of places all around the country, across the socioeconomic spectrum, all moving beyond midlife and reflecting on their odysseys. This book set out to impart their tales. I even thought of it as an homage to Studs Terkel's collection of first-person narratives, *Working*. My goal was to let them speak. But as the narratives piled up, the many stories—in all their idiosyncrasies—insisted on telling a larger tale.

The individual odysseys were part of a bigger migration—not only from one job to another but also from midlife to an emerging period between the middle years and anything resembling either retirement or old age. It's the story of a generation's movement into unfamiliar terrain, an often awkward adventure that carries with it the potential to be one of the greatest transformations of the twenty-first century.

UNSTABLE SPACE

What is it that I learned from these numerous conversations over many months? We need a new map of life. We've been making do with one that was fashioned for an expected longevity of threescore and ten. We shouldn't knock that legacy. At one time, that constituted progress. But we can't stuff a twenty-first-century life span into a life course designed for the twentieth century— or stretch the old model so that it accommodates a task well beyond its intended capacity. The story starts with the numbers, but it is really about the nature of lives.

In 1900, the life span in the United States was forty-seven. Today, it is approaching eighty (although great disparities persist across class and race). Overall, that's an increase in a hundred years approximating all the gains since the beginning of time. And the length of life may well be headed toward the century mark. Some think the upward rise will be even more precipitous.

Yet while we've been remarkably adept at extending lives, our imagination and innovation in remaking the shape of those longer lives have been struggling to keep pace. In the words of anthropologist Mary Catherine Bateson, we're "living longer and thinking shorter." The situation is beginning to fray, especially in the period of life that is emerging between traditional midlife and what used to be occupied by retirement and old age. It's fair to say that this condition constitutes a long-standing problem, one that existed even before longer lives and changing demographics made it a much bigger one. The territory between middle age and old age has long been shaky ground, "unstable social space," in the words of cultural historian Thomas Cole.

Remarkably, the first recipient of Social Security, a bookkeeper named Ida May Fuller, started to collect her checks in 1940. She proceeded to live another thirty-five years, long enough to witness the ascent and disbanding of the Beatles and the landing of the man on the moon. (For her total $24.75 contribution, she received $22,888.92 in benefits, perhaps qualifying her as the nation's first de facto lottery winner, as well as its inaugural Social Security recipient.)

Indeed, the time between the end of work and the end of life was already starting to raise uncomfortable questions in the decades following the establishment of Social Security and mass retirement—most fundamentally, what do you do with yourself during this period? Medical experts were advising a quiet existence, rocking peacefully in *Whistler's Mother*–like fashion. What role would this population in their sixties and beyond play in American life, especially as their numbers grew? How was it that increased economic security at the personal level was producing a purpose gap for many of those individuals, their growing years spent dangling, in what one scholar of the time called a "roleless role," on the margins of society? It's no wonder labor leader Walter Reuther described this period in 1949 as "too old to work, too young to die." It was a very awkward time, an "in-between" period.

It took ingenuity to redesign lives to keep up with changes in longevity and society in mid-twentieth-century America, but we rose to the occasion. We plugged the purpose gap with something called the "golden years," a stunning innovation that almost overnight turned an arid economic institution, retirement, from an anteroom to the great beyond into a core component of the American dream. We did such a good job of making virtue out of seeming necessity that soon retirement at sixty-five wasn't enough. Even as lives were already lengthening, we wanted retirement earlier and earlier. We couldn't wait to stop working and start playing in a period that was fashioned by financial marketers and housing entrepreneurs as a kind of second childhood. Golf became the new symbol of late-life success. A new deal was struck around shorter working lives that turned the push out of the labor market into a powerful pull. The golden years shored up the postmidlife purpose gap for fifty years and then some, filling the unstable space with something aspirational and attainable. This was a dream for average Americans, not just the elite. But as lives lengthened and careers shortened, this fix grew shakier and shakier, especially as the vast wave of boomers began approaching.

Kurt Andersen, in his book *Reset*, provides a useful context of broader changes in American life over the past quarter century. Andersen suggests that we are in the aftermath of what might be characterized as the bloating of America, a mass overextension that occurred between 1980 and the late 2000s. Mortgages mushroomed, debt ballooned, and our houses expanded, along with our waistlines. We could easily add the golden years to the package, as they went from an assumedly brief proposition at the end of life, a well-earned respite, to a thirty-year McMansion of a stage, inflated until it literally constituted the second *half* of adulthood. But it became both unattainable, for most individuals, and unsustainable, for a society soon to have more people over sixty than under fifteen. (And we're relatively young in the community of nations—Japan, South Korea, Germany, Italy, and Spain will see over-sixty populations approaching or exceeding 40 percent by the middle of the twenty-first century.)

Unsustainable and unattainable, the old dream dies hard, as a recent ad from Allstate illustrates. Advising readers to "consider this: Hallmark sold 85,000 'Happy 100th Birthday!' cards last year," the ad asks, "How long of a retirement *should you plan for*?" It then answers its own question. "The average 65-year-old woman can expect to live until 87, and the average 65-year-old man to 84. So it's easy to understand why workers today should plan for a 30-year retirement." It then concludes: "Let's save retirement by saving for retirement."

Thirty-year retirements, in the era of the Great Recession? Let's face it, that is simply not going to work, nor is it desirable. Does it make much sense for society to throw away the most experienced segment of the population when it is a long way from obsolescence?

This book argues that the way to make the most of coming hundred-year life spans is not to stretch and strain the contours of a life course set up for a bygone era. That's like plastic surgery to make a seventy-year-old face look like a forty-year-old one— the result is unnatural and the intention wrongheaded. Likewise, the answer to the unsustainability of thirty-year retirements is not substituting endless middle age for endless old age, the alternative some are proposing to the much longer life. Middle age, like all good things, eventually must reach an end. No use denying it. In Nora Ephron's words, "There's a moment when people know—whatever their skills are at denial—that they have passed from what they can delude themselves into thinking is middle age to something that you could call the third act." Ephron, now sixty-nine, declares, "I'm definitely in the third act."

As the "third act" notion suggests, the reality is that the end of middle age is no longer, for most people, attached to the beginning of either retirement or old age. (It's like the transcontinental railroad, started at both ends, designed to eventually meet. However, the two ends of this project—life—don't meet anymore.) Individuals left in that lurch, in this unstable space that has no name, no clear beginning or end, no rites or routes of passage, face a contradictory culture, incoherent policies, institutions tailored for a different population, and a society that seems in denial that this period even exists.

Daphne Merkin describes the unease of this predicament: "Sheer dread lies in wait: the fear that we're fast gaining upon that demarcation line where you stop being young and you start being something else entirely, someone belonging to a different order of nomenclature." Merkin adds, "Middle age becomes a life raft that we can't afford to fall off." Her observation is timely. We're in the early stages of a great migration, but it is not the old retiree migration that literally saw millions travel from north to south, from cold, drizzling places like Michigan and Pennsylvania and Oregon to warm, recreational states like Arizona and Florida.

The new migration is across time and the life course, as tens of millions (8,000 a day, one every ten seconds, are turning sixty) reach the spot where middle age used to end and old age once began, the new territory where a resurgent purpose gap, and gulf in identity, stands. Opportunity is there as well. The surge of people into this new stage of life is one of the most important social phenomena of the new century. Never before have so many people had so much experience and the time and the capacity to do something significant with it. That's the gift of longevity, the great potential payoff on all the progress we've made in extending lives. Realizing these possibilities will require the courage to break from old and familiar patterns that once were our friends but just don't work any longer.

This book is a plea for mustering the imagination and the will to forge a new map of life fitted to a new length of life and to the particular circumstances and opportunities of the twenty-first century. It argues for the creation of a new stage between the end of the middle years and the beginning of retirement and old age, an encore stage of life characterized by purpose, contribution, and commitment, particularly to the well-being of future generations.

The ensuing chapters seek to tell the stories of a new group of pioneers who aren't waiting for permission from anyone to begin fashioning this new phase. They are harbingers from a land that has yet to be realized, signals from a future we would be happy to inhabit. As the science fiction writer William Gibson states, that future is already here, "it's just unevenly distributed."

Throughout, the book is animated by a simple premise: that the challenge of transitioning to and making the most of this new stage—while deeply personal—is much more than an individual problem. As such, it's just too hard, the exclusive province of the heroic, lucky, or loaded. No glib talk from advicemongers or exhortations from the optimistic will do the trick. What we're facing is not a solo matter; it's a social imperative, an urgent one that must be solved as the great midlife migration gathers scale and momentum. Inventing a new stage of life is a conscious decision that won't happen by itself, easily or automatically, even as the soil becomes more fertile and conditions increasingly ripe. This book issues a call to action for creating the new stage and offers a set of prescriptions for realizing this opportunity.

If we act, the new stage could well become a destination, even the new crown of life, and the individuals flooding into it the human-capital solution to much that ails us in this society. As we confront significant challenges in areas like education, the environment, and health care, this windfall of talent could help carry us toward a new generation of solutions. We are in the position to make a monument from what used to be the leftover years, a second chance for people of all stripes to ascend the ladder of contribution and fulfillment, and an opportunity for society to "grow up" along with its population. This amounts to nothing less than changing the pattern of lives, and with it the nature and possibilities of every stage along the way. It's time, once again, to rise to the occasion. It's time for a shift—a shift in thinking and in culture, in social institutions and public policies, a shift from what worked in the past to what can carry us into the future.

TWO

One River at a Time

....

Joseph Campbell said midlife is when you get to the top of the ladder and discover it is leaning against the wrong wall. He remarked that one sees these people all the time, the ones who are perched on the wrong ladder, who set out with big dreams but either failed to pursue them or were thwarted in their efforts to do so. In Campbell's words, "They have not lived their lives."

When Meredith McKenzie got up at her fiftieth birthday party, she announced that she was not living the life she wanted. She had been battered by a series of setbacks. It was time to take a step back, reassess the direction of her life, hit the reset button. She announced that she would be moving from the Los Angeles area to tiny Kernville, in the southern Sierra Nevada, where her late husband's family owned a small house. "I ran away from home," she says now about this period.

McKenzie admits that most of her friends and family thought she was crazy, or else having a midlife crisis. She certainly had weathered a series of crises in midlife. In 1998 her life "blew up." Her husband, only fifty-one, died suddenly. That alone would have been enough to send anyone reeling. However, the same year she fell off a horse and shattered her hip, leaving McKenzie horizontal for months. It was like instant old age. She recalls that it took hours each morning just to get out of bed and go through the process of dressing herself. The third shock was less visceral but equally devastating. Growing up in a working-class family outside of Youngstown, Ohio, in the 1950s and 1960s (her father was a toolmaker), McKenzie dreamed of being a lawyer, in the spirit of Clarence Darrow or Thurgood Marshall. Her plan was clear: go to college, go to law school, go to work on the great issues of the time, like civil rights.

It didn't work out that way. Pregnant and married at twenty-two, she felt obliged to pursue the more practical route of a communications degree, which led McKenzie to Los Angeles to work on the production side of commercial and public television shows. Later, as a single mother, she studied at night for a real estate license, to get more flexibility to spend time around her daughter as she grew up.

When her daughter left the house, McKenzie got right back to her plan, applying to law school, going to Loyola full time with students half her age, graduating three years later. But this didn't go according to plan, either. It was increasingly clear to her that the dream deferred was not the dream she'd harbored. The desultory practice of law she encountered in summer jobs and other experience was a far cry from the crusading social justice work she'd envisioned. When McKenzie failed the bar by a narrow margin, it was personally difficult, accompanied by feelings of failure. But it was also confirmation that this chapter wasn't working.

The death of a husband, a crippling injury, and the collapse of a lifelong dream (at the price of tens of thousands in tuition and fees, not to mention three years of life) produced a kind of white-flag moment for McKenzie. "It was my year of agony," she says now. Then, basically, she said, "Enough!"

In going to Kernville—a rural refuge she'd visited regularly over the years—McKenzie created her own gap year, which turned out to be a two-year retreat, from 2002 through 2004. McKenzie says today that they were the happiest years of her life. They provided new perspective, and physical and spiritual renewal, in a peaceful and bucolic setting. The gap period also led, much to her surprise, to a new direction for her life.

McKenzie had always spent time, recreationally, around rivers. Coming back to Kernville was, in her words, a "homecoming" (really, she ran away *to* home, not *from* it). In Kernville she started doing more than appreciating nature and rivers as a source of play. Angered by encroachment on the river environment by housing developers, she began working on protection and restoration issues, initially as a volunteer and later as a consultant. In the process McKenzie discovered she was using her legal knowledge, her real estate savvy, her lifelong love of water and the outdoors. She decided she wanted to refocus her life on river conservation and restoration.

Harvard sociologist Sara Lawrence-Lightfoot describes the interconnected impulses of "looking back" and "giving forward" in her book *The Third Chapter*, based on many interviews she did with individuals at the same life point as Meredith McKenzie. McKenzie reached back to the past, integrating long-standing interests and accumulated skills to come up with a sense of "what's next," one that ripened into the future direction for her life.

That said, the process for her has been fitful. Instead of following her espoused direction after Kernville, McKenzie, remarkably, headed backward, back to the Los Angeles area, *and back to the real estate business*, where for two and a half years she not only sold real estate but also managed an agency with sixty agents reporting to her. It was stressful, hectic, and intense. The job taught her how to manage a business, but it ran counter to everything she had concluded about herself during the time in Kernville and everything she had determined she would do with the rest of her life.

What happened? "I panicked. Really, I relapsed—it was like I was in recovery in Kernville, and then I relapsed." Her funds were running low, the soaring real estate market beckoned, McKenzie's daughter had met a "wonderful man," and she could tell a wedding (with attendant costs) was coming. In the end, McKenzie says, she was a typical boomer in the throes of boom time. There are many like her, she says. "We like to live large. We're very competitive. And I was no different than anybody else." She adds, "I think I bought into something that everybody bought into, which is a definition of the American Dream as being more, more, more, more, more; and an economic society that said grow, grow, grow, grow, grow."

Now McKenzie describes the return to real estate as her "detour." She ended up living in a big house near the beach, wining and dining clients over lunch, generally living the high life. Then the downturn hit, and she realized that she was not only an active agent of the real estate spiral, part of a system putting people into houses they often couldn't afford, but also a victim—struggling to pay her own monthly costs at a time when making money selling houses was becoming virtually impossible. The detour had run its course, and then some. McKenzie kept asking herself, more and more insistently, "When are you going to start living your life?"

So this time, Meredith McKenzie blew up her own life, perhaps in anticipation of a coming collapse. She traded the expansive house for a three-hundred-square-foot converted garage, living like a grad student, maybe an undergrad. She swapped the boom-time lifestyle for an ascetic existence akin to the one she'd grown accustomed to in Kernville, and she jettisoned the six-figure real estate job to look for work doing river restoration, knowing at best she'd make a fraction of her former salary.

To McKenzie's amazement, things seemed to be working out. She answered a Craigslist ad and was hired by the Arroyo Seco Foundation in Pasadena as a watershed-restoration program manager. The salary wasn't much, but she was thrilled. At long last her life was taking on a kind of alignment. And unlike the dream of a legal career, she actually enjoyed doing this work. It felt like a true calling.

Stop here and you've got another lovely, seamless tale of boomer reinvention gone right—cue the singing birds, the parting clouds, another triumph for the American belief in glorious rebirth. Furthermore, it's one particularly suited to the era of renewed interest in sustainability. Here is a woman who abandoned the world of selling sprawl and living large for a more sustainable lifestyle conducted on a tiny footprint—accompanied by an adoring dog—all the while sustaining herself through paid employment working directly on issues of river restoration.

Add a sense of balance. McKenzie estimates that her anxiety level dropped "about 90 percent" in her new job and lifestyle. "When you're stressing out trying to figure out how you're going to make your nut of $6,500 a month while you're watching your opportunity to make money drop, that's extremely stressful. And all I can say is . . . it's really liberating."

That description is appealing. But it's just too easy. The change in life directions is usually much messier in real life than in magazine features. And the experience of downshifting for McKenzie was wrenching. Moving into a garage at fifty-five is not like moving from your parents' to a dorm room, or for that matter from a dorm room to a garage. Early on, McKenzie reflects, "I actually one night sat down and cried and said, 'What have I done? What have I done? Oh my goodness.'" Friends and family were worried about her, once again convinced she was having a midlife crisis. She faced bouts of profound self-doubt. Was this any way to be approaching her sixtieth birthday?

And that was a relatively high point. Within months of making her big shift, the same forces feeding the housing collapse were squeezing the California state budget, the main source of funding for the Arroyo Seco Foundation. After state funds evaporated, McKenzie lost her position. At first she moved into a consulting role. Soon that too dried up.

McKenzie regrouped, cobbling together a portfolio comprised of consulting on water law and environmental planning, with a part-time teaching gig on that subject at the California State Polytechnic University, Pomona, and a new real estate practice on the side, this time specializing in clients interested in living green and buying houses that fitted those aspirations. She is once again using all her skills—legal, real estate, communications—in service of a new goal, that of environmental preservation and education. She's even created a course on sustainable development for the local board of realtors.

McKenzie remains committed to—one might say enraptured with—the Arroyo Seco. That love has not departed with the job. She writes a blog under the handle "Arroyolover." Her e-mail address is "arroyolover@." She even believes that the move back to the Los Angeles area, for all its ups and downs, was a kind of disguised blessing, since McKenzie now feels that the real challenge facing rivers is the behavior of the residents who live near them. There are some 200,000 people living adjacent to the Arroyo Seco alone.

Throughout, McKenzie has also come to embody what *Bloomberg Businessweek* columnist Chris Farrell calls the New Frugality, a marriage of virtue and necessity, of living inexpensively with living green. The inexpensive part has been critical. That's what has enabled her to have extra freedom, to handle the vicissitudes of "starting from ground zero" in her sustainability career, including the reality of age discrimination, which she feels as strongly from nonprofits and government agencies as from private businesses. Also, a key ingredient to being a pioneer embarking

on an encore in a new stage of life has been "not having responsibility for another human being," now that her daughter is grown
up. Indeed, McKenzie is now the grandmother of a two-year-old,
an important part of her life these days.

She admits that perhaps she *overdownsized*. That said, she's
guarding against future detours and relapses: "I will do whatever
I have to do to do this work. If that means for a couple of years
I have to live like a nun, then I will live like a nun, because this
is the work I want to do the rest of my life."

I asked her about the idea that this is a midlife crisis, maybe
a recurring one. She shakes her head. Looking over her "mean-
dering" path, she tries to put her transition today into perspective: "I've lived a pretty conventional life. What I've gotten to do
in my fifties is what a lot of people did in their twenties and early
thirties. I wasn't having a midlife crisis. I was just now doing that
self-exploration that a lot of young people get to do."

Besides, she has time on her side. It's the "halfway point" in
adulthood, she says. Her father lived to ninety, and her mother
is still going strong at eighty-nine. And that will come in
handy—the do-it-yourself (DIY) process of changing one's life
as a late fiftysomething is like "starting a new business, like being
an entrepreneur." Actually, that's not exactly it, in her view: "It's
like walking the high trapeze without a net." Indeed, in the entrepreneurial spirit, McKenzie's now thinking about starting an
organization, the Urban River Institute, and writing a book
about her passion. It's going to be called *One River at a Time*.

On the last day of summer 2009, I traveled to Los Angeles to talk with McKenzie one more time, after many months of phone conversations. She picked me up in front of my hotel to make the eleven-mile sojourn down the Arroyo Seco—from the rural setting where it emerges from the San Gabriel Mountains until it empties into the Los Angeles River in a concrete viaduct behind a neighborhood filled with fast-food restaurants and check-cashing booths. The trip takes less than an hour, traffic included.

As we pause toward the end of the tour, with Confluence Park, a recreational area with rail and communication lines converging around us, Dodger Stadium and Elysian Park looming just above, and the Arroyo Seco running through it all, McKenzie admits that she doesn't really expect to achieve the overall goal of restoring the Arroyo Seco during her lifetime, even if it's just one river, even if she does manage once again to make it a full-time job. Is she discouraged about that? Does she ever think about throwing in the towel? "If I see one of these major points that I showed you restored, before I die," she reflects, as we get back in the car and drive through an alley lined by warehouses, "then it's worthwhile, all the sacrifices, all the living like a nun." She pauses. "If my granddaughter, who is two-years-old, sees the steelhead trout going up and down this river again—and when I say, 'If she sees it,' I mean she's not going to see it when she's twenty, either—but if she sees it by the time she's fifty, then I've done my job." Her words remind me of a Greek proverb: "A society grows great when old men plant trees in whose shade they know they shall never sit"—or when not nearly old women restore rivers in which they will never play, but their grand-daughters might.

McKenzie's reflections have a lot to say about the nature of sustainability. The river might be tangible, eleven miles long with a beginning, middle, and end. That's a manageable project. It's also timeless. It needs to be maintained and nurtured across generations. The combination is appealing. It contributes to McKenzie's many-faceted commitment to sustainability, including her new lifestyle of frugality and restoration work.

She's doing something else as well: charting a more enduring vision of the life course, a human sustainability that's akin to its environmental counterpart, one that refuses to confine and overload everyone's productive contributions in the first half of life and then throw away our capacities and passions prematurely, long before they're used up. That's something to be passed on as well, to those future generations poised to live out lives far longer than our own.

THREE

A World Out of Whack

....

It's no surprise that friends and family were worried that Meredith McKenzie's big shift was in fact some sort of variation on the stereotypical midlife crisis. Here's a woman in her fifties, whose growing discontent over job, lifestyle, and questions of deeper meaning helps prompt a dramatic life makeover, one that connects back to her youth and earlier dreams. McKenzie herself avoids the crisis interpretation. She sees herself moving into the second half of adulthood, experiencing the "self-exploration" typical of one's twenties in her fifties. What's the rush, with thirty or more years to go?

I don't see a classic midlife crisis in McKenzie's story, either. To my mind she's at the vanguard of navigating a much larger transition, as *millions* of people in their fifties and sixties grapple with essential questions about their lives and their futures, while simultaneously attempting to make sense of an outdated life course stretching midlife or retirement beyond recognition.

Still, when we see middle-aged turmoil, the classic midlife crisis is our lens of least resistance. The crisis has become an American cultural tradition—even if the concept was invented by a Canadian, psychologist Elliott Jaques, who coined the phrase in his 1965 *International Journal of Psychoanalysis* article, "Death and the Midlife Crisis." Studying hundreds of artists, writers, and other creative geniuses, Jaques defined the crisis as "the adult encounter with the conception of life to be lived in the setting of an approaching personal death." Some of these artists did in fact die shortly thereafter. Others hit a creative wall and never did significant work again.

As the midlife crisis itself approaches its own fiftieth birthday, Jaques's phrase not only persists but seems to be spreading. The popular features of the classic midlife crisis remain the same: a desperate grasp for lost youth, dramatic life changes, makeovers in appearance (oftentimes involving assistance from products and scalpels), trading in one's spouse for a newer model, and rejection of work that's becoming numbing and meaningless, to veer off in an often inexplicable direction.

The crisis, originated in a study of artists, is itself the subject of much art and pop culture. Every decade seems to produce its own archetypal tale of the midlife crisis, helping keep it in the popular mind. Sam Mendes's 1999 midlife crisis masterwork, *American Beauty*, chronicles the trials of middle-aged Lester Burnham, stuck in a job he hates, trapped in an unhappy marriage, sinking into an abyss of self-loathing. Burnham's passion is awakened by a high school cheerleader. It all ends badly.

The tradition continues in *Men of a Certain Age*, Ray Romano's television series about three college friends approaching their fiftieth birthdays and, according to the show's marketing materials, "experiencing the changes and challenges of mid-life" and "navigating through the second act of their lives." One advertisement for the series, which premiered in December 2009, asks the question, "Are you just getting started or half-finished?" The show seems to lean toward the latter. Critic Jeff Roush dubs the show *Sad Men*, in contrast to *Mad Men*.

Ray Romano has commented that the show reflects his own experience of hitting fifty and thinking, "What is this foreign land I'm in?" adding, "It was my version of a midlife crisis of 'What's next?'" Likewise, Romano's fiftysomething cowriter, Mike Royce, recalls the idea for the series germinating in his own life. He remembers wondering: "How many more days am I going to feel young and vibrant?"

From these examples and Jaques's history, one might think the crisis to be the restricted domain of struggling middle-aged men. To be sure, men have been the focus of much of what's been written for decades about mayhem in the middle years. But *Wall Street Journal* columnist Sue Shellenbarger's 2005 book, *The Breaking Point: How Today's Women Are Navigating the Midlife Crisis*, brought gender balance to the domain. In it Shellenbarger describes her own descent into increasingly reckless behavior, some of it behind the wheel of an all-terrain vehicle, until she so badly breaks her collarbone that she's physically disfigured and forced to halt. Her crisis is precipitated by the death of her father and accentuated by a divorce and other unfinished business.

The book argues that the midlife crisis is a widespread phenomenon among American women today and sketches a set of archetypes women can use to turn the crisis into an opportunity.

It was followed by a *Time* cover story proclaiming, "A Female Midlife Crisis? Bring It On!" For comic relief, *Time*'s story features a cartoon, "Hey, They Stole Our Crisis," portraying two midlife men lamenting that it wasn't enough for women to want to join country clubs and be on the Supreme Court; now they were determined to take away the middle-aged man's last bastion: the midlife crisis. "Don't we get ANYTHING to ourselves?" one complains.

The contours of the crisis are by no means confined to the popular press. Bronwyn Fryer, a former editor at the *Harvard Business Review*, describes this state as "career menopause," and not just for women. "Night sweats. Heart palpitations. Crying jags. Mood swings. I'm a 55-year-old woman, well and gratefully past that hormonal 'change of life.' So what the heck was this thing?'" she writes. When a younger colleague gives her the career-menopause frame, it fits like a glove. "I've always loved my job, but for ages I've been feeling something else—call it a longing for greater self-fulfillment—tugging at me. Relatives and friends have had brushes with death, or have died. I, too, have felt the shadow of my own mortality. I've been aching to write The Great American Novel, or volunteer for the Peace Corps, or sing in my band, or do some other as-yet-undefined-thing—before it's too late."

So, for men *and* women these days, the midlife-crisis drama has staying power, despite considerable skepticism by researchers trying to assess its very existence. A major MacArthur Foundation research initiative from the 1990s found, for example, that while everyone recognizes the term *midlife crisis*, only a small fraction of individuals surveyed feel they've had one. Why, then, does the notion continue to flourish in the popular culture, the advice literature, and the world of arts, movies, novels, even management thinking—though relatively few experience anything literally resembling the classic form of the crisis? The reason, I believe, is that it's a good story—dramatizing concerns on the minds of many.

As a growing group of individuals move through middle age, they are much more likely to confront the inescapable reality that we don't live forever, as Bronwyn Fryer underscores. Mortality stands near the core of every midlife-crisis tale. Many are likewise grappling with what it means to no longer be young, in a society extraordinarily wedded to the idea of endless youth. And the midlife-crisis myth further touches on the anxiety that this period raises for many facing a crossroads—completing one chapter yet unsure about how to set out on the next. Taken together, the midlife-crisis fable captures all these anxieties and tells a story about them, one that more and more individuals can relate to, as more and more men and women move into a new and ill-charted phase of life.

THE NEW MIDLIFE CHASM

In truth, it's possible to think of two simultaneous midlife "crises" present in America today. They are more accurately challenges about what follows the middle years as tens of thousands move into their fifties and sixties each day. The first one, described above, is internal—the stuff of psyche and spirit, more reflective of the big issues facing those hitting this period than any literal living out of the *American Beauty* experience. The second one is external and structural. It's often obscured by the first, the classic midlife tale of existential upheaval. Driving forward, the external version is the longevity revolution, which is creating a significant period of time between the middle years and old age.

In the past, individuals moving beyond midlife might have proceeded directly into the social institution called retirement—or, if that was delayed, tread water for a couple of years before ducking into that safe harbor of identity and security. Today they are, for the most part, on their own, in uncharted waters, facing fundamental questions about what's next and what matters along with a society unprepared for them. An array of difficulties looms ahead.

One might argue they face a midlife *chasm* even more than a crisis. This gulf recalls an ad from the Principal Financial Group in the style of a *New Yorker* cartoon. The drawing depicts two areas of solid ground, one labeled "Work," the other "Retirement," with a gap opened between them. Catapulting across the void is the cartoon's hero, an everyman of a certain age perched on a bicycle, replete with receding hairline and visible paunch. The caption underneath the drawing asks, "Need a Lift?" Making it across this divide, the text continues, "can seem like a pretty daunting task. What do you do? How much should you save? Where do you begin?"

The Principal ad appeared just before the downturn, and it suggests some patches are required in the familiar procession of the life course. Instead of the seamless shift from midlife work to leisured retirement that has long been the norm, new circumstances require adaptation, it suggests. Sociologist Phyllis Moen of the University of Minnesota calls this mentality "the norm—postponed." Mind the gap, and everything will go according to the familiar plan.

But in truth, the experience depicted in the Principal ad is rapidly disappearing. If it were to reflect emerging reality, the illustration would probably require a two-page spread—to approximate the vast stretch that's opened up between the familiar stages. Maybe Principal would be supplying its cartoon character with a telescope instead of a ramp.

The intervening space is not just wide; it's confusing and chaotic, a mismatched mess of mixed signals, outdated norms, anachronistic institutions, and multiple misperceptions. A series of troubling features characterize this growing chasm—a void in individual identity, an absence of coherent institutions (and policies), and a lack of understanding about what's happening more broadly to the society. Together these gaps and gulfs threaten to transform a breathtaking opportunity into a seemingly insurmountable problem.

The Oxymoronic Years

In Greek *oxymoron* translates to "pointedly foolish." The dictionary defines it as "a combination of contradictory or incongruous words." That definition pretty well characterizes the cultural, institutional, and policy landscape awaiting those in the great midlife migration, confronting language and experiences fashioned for an earlier generation that often make little sense today, an *Alice in Wonderland* world where words and meaning collapse on each other, where, for example, work and its opposite, retirement, are jammed together and some are referred to as the "young old." Life as an incongruity. It's a sure sign that something entirely new is in the offing, but in the interim it's both confounding and deflating.

One common new-stage oxymoron is *working retired*, coined by no less a wordsmith than Mark Penn, the author of *Microtrends*. Penn heads Burson-Marsteller, the giant PR firm. He did a marvelous piece of phrase making in coming up with the *soccer moms* moniker. However, if *working retired* is the best Penn can do—it's hard to imagine anyone looking forward to, planning for, and investing in being "working retired" (how about "walking dead"?)—it's evident that the challenge of naming this time of life is formidable.

And it's not just the phrase. Echoes of the "working retired" notion are easy to spot. Consider that the word *retirement* itself derives from the Middle French meaning of "to go off into seclusion"—at the very least to go out of the workplace. Then consider the December 2009 issue of the magazine *Where to Retire*. On the cover are two fit and classically good-looking retirees from Colorado Springs, along with their golden retriever, poised on a bluff with a magnificent natural landscape behind them. Dwarfing this typical retirement image is the banner heralding the issue's cover story: "8 Enticing Cities for New Careers." That's the cover story of a retirement magazine.

The October 2010 issue of *U.S. News & World Report* featured a cover story, "How to Retire Smart: What You Need to Know to Get the Most Out of Your Retirement." The lead story: "Top Spots for a Second Career." The March 2010 issue of the *New York Times* special section called "Retirement" featured two stories on its cover. One was about people starting new businesses and organizations, the other about the fields where job growth is projected in the coming decade. Language and reality remain at oxymoronic odds.

In the summer of 2010 I had the chance to participate on a Merrill Lynch–sponsored panel called "Second Acts," featuring videos of three customers of the firm: one a former corporate CEO heading up an economic development organization in Detroit; another a career military officer, who has since started four new businesses in Atlanta, working together with his wife; and a couple in Texas who had "retired" to run a farm and a cooking school on the property. The message of the otherwise-excellent Merrill Lynch initiative—"Help2Retire"—formed the backdrop behind me.

The following month I found myself testifying in front of the U.S. Senate's esteemed Finance Committee, originator of the G.I. Bill and other landmark legislation. The title of the hearing, itself an important step in helping to advance policy debate around longer contributing lives, was "Choosing to Work During Retirement and the Impact on Social Security."

Oxymorons like *working retired* and its various manifestations can't help but convey a two-dimensional, split-difference sense of this period that suggests half of one thing, half of the other: halfway in, halfway out; halfway capable, halfway committed. They further intimate that this is a transitional phase, a bridge between real categories—like work and retirement. No surprise that individuals seen as "working retired" might face skepticism from employers wondering how long they are going to stay, how committed they are to their jobs, or whether they are just passing through en route to the intended destination of retirement.

If *working retired* is one of the common contradictory couplings today, *young old* stands at the top of the oxymoronic order, a term of choice for many social scientists, particularly those from the field of aging. (It should probably be no surprise that if your field is aging, you see people as various flavors of aging.)

Writing in the British medical journal *The Lancet*, researchers Kaare Christensen, James Vaupel, and colleagues deliver the remarkable projection that "most babies born since 2000 in France, Germany, Italy, the UK, the USA, Canada, Japan, and other countries with long life expectancies will celebrate their 100th birthdays." That prompts them to the following conclusion, among others, about the implication of these longer lives: "Traditionally, man has three major periods of life: childhood, adulthood, and old age. Old age is now evolving into two segments," which they characterize as "young old" and "oldest old." The young old? Are most people in their fifties and sixties in anything resembling "old age"? Are they elderly? Senior citizens? Much more likely their parents are approaching that period. (Why not *child old* for those in their forties, *infant old* for the late-thirties set, *prenatal old* for latter twentysomethings?)

Yet the young-old label is increasingly widespread, another split difference that suggests a transitory period between real and substantial stages. Jack Rosenthal, the Pulitzer Prize–winning former editor of the *New York Times* editorial page, sums up the linguistic state of things when he remarks simply, "Language has not yet caught up with life."

Lost Youth and Premature Aging

The "young-old" label suggests halfway status, a limbo land somewhere between the poles of the age spectrum. However, this characterization also evokes a powerful and contradictory tension facing many moving beyond the midlife years. On the one hand, there are cultural and social pressures to hang on to one's youth, a powerful pull in a society obsessed with and reverential about being young. On the other hand, there is an equal push to brand us as older than we are.

It's ironic that, as a start-up nation, in the seventeenth and eighteenth centuries, America was a "gerontocracy" that upheld and glorified being *old*. In a society where few lived beyond thirty or forty, those who made it that far were seen as closer to God, and their longevity was viewed as a sign from the divine. People actually tried to look older than they were. They wore white wigs and cut their clothes so they appeared hunched over. They lied on the census, claiming to be a few years older than they actually were!

Today's truth is, obviously, different. Botox is a multibillion-dollar industry. Hair-coloring sales are in the hundreds of millions annually. Job-search experts counsel those over fifty on clever ways to hide their ages in job applications and to dumb down their experience on their résumés. We regularly hear, as already stated, triumphant pronouncements that fifty is the new thirty, sixty the new forty, and various other combinations underscoring the goal of youth.

We haven't been content just trying to make younger versions of our adult selves. A major part of the retirement culture over the past fifty years has been to turn the period after sixty into a second childhood. "Twice a child, once a man," said Shakespeare, referring to the childlike tendencies of the very old. Had he lived in contemporary America, he would have felt vindicated. Just think of the names of places like Leisure World, which are adult playgrounds designed to support a second childhood built around play.

The financial-services marketing literature—a particular fascination of mine—pushes this idea unapologetically. One ad from the Hartford insurance company literally announces, "We don't know when childhood ends, but it starts again at retirement." Their two-page spread in the *New York Times Magazine* continues, in smaller print, in case anyone missed the message the first time around, "Retirement. Time once again to play." Or this from Ameriprise, featuring a couple of seven-year-olds playing pirate: "Retirement is like a second childhood."

The signs extend well past financial-services propaganda. *Time* offers this headline: "How Not to Look Old on the Job: More Boomers Are Working into Their Senior Years, and Who Wants to Look Like the Office Geezer?" It goes on to report that the anti-aging business is now a $50 billion sector annually. Under the headline "New Ways to Tap into the Fountain of Youth," *Time* looks at the benefits, procedures, and costs of tooth lengthening (I thought being long of tooth was a sign of aging), butt lifts and implants, neck tucks, knee tightening, hair restoration, earlobe repair, and "extreme hand makeover." The writer, Christopher Noxon, describes the overall phenomenon of adults who try either to look or to act much younger by calling them "rejuveniles." Yet while there are abundant signals telling us to be younger than we are—rejuveniles, perhaps—the opposite is also true. Myriad messages subtle and otherwise inform us that, like it or not, we're older than we actually are—signs of what might be called "premature aging."

This book started with my tale of getting a senior discount (along with two cribs) at a hotel at age fifty. Likewise, we find ourselves at fifty in the crosshairs not only for AARP (formerly known as the American Association of Retired Persons until it became clear that much of their membership was not retired at all), for senior centers looking to attract the boomers, and for elder learning programs, but also for adventure brochures aimed at the leisure set. Under the jurisdiction of Administrations on Aging and Departments of Elder Affairs, we're even a protected class in the labor market—mature workers (and given age discrimination, it's a good thing, too). Opportunities for senior discounts beyond those offered by AARP proliferate; one need look no further than the local movie theater for that awkward decision about whether one takes the two bucks off for the price of confessing to a false label.

Glance at newspaper headlines about the boomers, and we're described as graybeards and geezers, when in many cases our parents barely qualify for those descriptors. And we're not talking about the supermarket tabloids—two *New York Times* columns in recent years about boomers (approximately the age of the columnists who wrote them) were labeled "Geezers Doing Good" and "The Geezers' Crusade." *Fast Company* magazine describes a new leadership program at Harvard for those leaving midlife executive careers as "Blue-Hair University." It's not that it is insulting; it's just that, in truth, our teenage children have a much better chance of coming home with blue hair than we do. This truly is a world out of whack.

The DIY Life Stage

Passing through the airport I caught a summer 2010 cover story in *Esquire*, targeted toward men, titled "An Owner's Manual" and filled with age-specific tips on how to live healthfully and well. The cover trumpets: "A Guide to Your 20s, 30s, 40s, 50s," continuing: "After That, You're on Your Own." How true. For those entering the extended period between middle age and old age, finding your footing is a do-it-yourself process. Few role models for navigating this terrain exist; just as important, there is a paucity of institutions or policies. We are often faced with the choice of adapting the vehicles designed primarily for youth or consigning ourselves to the senior fare. Neither is the best fit.

The issue, in other words, is not just one of an oxymoronic identity or the contradictory cultural injunctions to hang on to lost youth or hang it up and accept premature labeling as old. It's a question of making these choices on our own, figuring things out for the most part one individual at a time, even while millions are facing the same challenges.

Should it be any surprise that the population that has no name, that is living out the category that doesn't exist, should be missing the social institutions, public policies, and transitional vehicles fitted to a new reality? Most conspicuously missing are the rites and the routes of passage to carry us from one stage to another.

Just think of this in contrast to retirement, where we've been spectacularly successful over much of the past fifty years inventing a coherent system in which culture, markets, organizations, and policies came together to create a powerful deal around shorter working lives and a recreational vision of the good life after sixty—an arrangement including everything from retirement communities through pensions and IRAs, to planning seminars and lifelong learning programs, even rites of passage like the gold watch and the retirement party. There has likewise been a significant policy investment—fraying today—along with a whole host of groups advocating on behalf of this segment. That was all cooked up in a half century to ease the passage into the golden years and make that period as fulfilling and secure as possible.

The comparison with youth is also instructive. The late Daniel Boorstin, distinguished American historian and former librarian of Congress, contrasts the predicament facing those who want to live lives of contribution and significance after fifty or sixty with our approach to individuals starting out earlier in life: "Our American strength, we have often been told, has been our youth. Ours is, or until recently was, a young nation. . . . It was the young in spirit, we say, who had the strength and the will and the flexibility to leave an Old World, to risk an Atlantic or Pacific passage for the uncertain promises of a still uncharted America." Boorstin points out that this has not just been an ethos: "We have been ingenious, too, in devising institutions—like our Land Grant colleges and the G.I. Bill—to make the best use of our youth resources."

When it comes to the postmidlife period, the prospects are dramatically different: "As our nation has matured—some would say only aged . . . our ingenuity in meeting the needs and opportunities and demands of youth has not been matched by any similar ingenuity" in engaging an older population. "The most conspicuous American institution directed" toward this group, in Boorstin's view, is "the so-called Leisure City, a place not of creation but of recreation and vegetation." Boorstin concludes with a call to develop a new generation of institutions "to employ the special talents and resources" of the most experienced segment of society. That task remains to be accomplished.

Reinvention Convention

Meanwhile, in the add-insult-to-injury category, as individuals are thrown into an identity chasm, buffeted between the poles of lost youth and premature aging, and then left largely alone to make it all up on their own, they are subjected to the ever-present myth of reinvention. In reality, this fantasy is a close cousin of the DIY experience, one that says it's all about heroic efforts and solo undertakings. If we are to believe what we read, boomers are annoyingly reinventing everything, most of all themselves.

Take *More* magazine, one of the great success stories in addressing the "certain age" crowd, a magazine that has managed to attract a million subscribers with slogans like "Share Your Wisdom, Live Your Passion, Show Your Style." Still, the magazine is built around a euphoric faith in radical reinvention. "Reinvent Yourself" is a major theme for the magazine and its Web site, with Reinvention Story Contests and even an annual Reinvention Convention.

More is hardly alone. The self-help shelves are crammed with books beckoning boomers to rise like phoenixes from the ashes of their earlier lives—through exercise plans, fad diets, and other offerings that hold the promise of personal transformation. (I admit, I'm guilty, too. An earlier book of mine was titled *Prime Time: How Baby Boomers Will Revolutionize Retirement and Transform America.*)

For all its resonance with long-standing themes in American culture—America itself broke free from the confines of the Old World in a kind of rebirth—the reinvention myth reinforces the idea that if we just try hard enough, think the right (positive) thoughts, and dream big dreams, we can engineer a magical escape from who we've been our whole lives—emerging as new, improved, and utterly distinct creatures (soon to be opening that bucolic vineyard or thriving alpaca farm without ever breaking a sweat, at least according to the money magazines). From my conversations over the years, I've become convinced the whole reinvention fantasy is part of the problem, that it constitutes an unrealistic expectation that only makes the fitful and usually murky process of transition to a new period in life all the more daunting—and contributes to a sense of failure if one falls short of achieving magical transformation, in short order.

It's Not Aging . . .

Personal reinvention isn't the only misconception inhibiting progress. More broadly, we suffer from a chasm of misunderstanding about the very nature of the demographic shift currently under way. Over and over again we are informed through the media and experts that the boomers are aging, that American society is in the midst of being engulfed in a gray wave. It's a version of the premature-aging distortion, extended from the individual level to society as a whole.

For more than a decade we've heard one jeremiad after another about the coming cataclysm, as the world is awash in mass codgerdom, bankrupting future generations, overstressing the health care system, and generally feeding a generational war favoring the old and compromising the young. At the heart of this perspective is what might be termed *scenario planning through the rearview mirror*—the easy coupling of the coming demographics (with more than a fifth of the United States, and a far greater proportion of Europe and Asia, moving toward their sixtieth birthdays) with the assumption that these individuals will continue the lifestyles, work patterns, health needs, and life-stage status of past generations (think: Florida and Arizona bursting at the seams with plaid-clad duffers).

This is shaky history—those patterns of the last generation themselves started changing dramatically in the latter part of the twentieth century. It's also bad scenario planning, exacerbated by an outlook of inevitability, the view that demography is destiny. These perspectives ignore essential reality: The *nature* of the postfifty period is under every bit as radical a revision as the *numbers*.

If you want to witness scenario planning through that rearview mirror, pick up a copy of the January–February 2010 issue of *Foreign Affairs*, a highly respected journal featuring the leading global minds dissecting important issues. Yet the cover story of this issue, blaring from sizable red type, is "The New Population Bomb," by Jack Goldstone, a professor at George Mason University. One of the big four "megatrends" constituting the coming bomb, according to Goldstone, is "aging pains." Goldstone starts off reciting the usual numbers of people who will be over sixty in the developed world. The article contains statements like this one: "As workers born during the baby boom of 1945–1965 are retiring they are not being replaced by a new cohort of citizens of prime working age (15–59 years old). Industrialized countries are experiencing a drop in their working age populations." Or this assertion, "By 2050, in other words, the entire working-age population will barely exceed the 60-and-older population."

To be fair, Goldstone goes on to suggest that policy makers take advantage of the longevity bonus and make it easier for individuals to work beyond sixty. Still, the notion that the "prime working years" are fifteen to fifty-nine and that sixty and beyond are no longer the "working years" leads to great distortions. Maybe that was true in 1950, but it certainly isn't inherently the case in 2010, and will seem even more anachronistic in 2050.

Language trails reality, and, I would add, understanding trails as well. Or to put it differently: these assumptions are extraordinarily arbitrary.

Economist Laurence Kotlikoff, in his book *The Coming Generational Storm*, cowritten with journalist Scott Burns, offers another vivid example of this outdated mind-set. In the book Kotlikoff and Burns predict that by 2030, when "77 million baby boomers hobble into old age, walkers will outnumber strollers," leading to what they describe as "fiscal child abuse." In 2030 I'll be seventy-two, and the youngest boomers will be sixty-six. It's possible that all 77 million of us will be perched on our walkers, but the truth is that the assumption is much more based on a mid-twentieth-century—make that mid-nineteenth-century—reality. More scenario planning through the back window.

One sees these kinds of predictions littered throughout the popular press and the pundit ranks where the "aging of the boomers," the "retirement of the boomers," and various predictions of population bombs, silver tsunamis, gray quakes, and other longevity- and demography-born disasters are repeated as fact because at one time in history sixty-year-olds were a prime market for walkers. A stock in trade of this thinking is the dependency ratio, built on anachronistic ideas like a working-age population that's fifteen to fifty-nine or sixty-five and notions of "retirement age" that simply no longer apply. Demographers likewise talk in grave tones about the "elder share," the segment of a nation's population over sixty, using this share as a marker of how decrepit the population is. It's no surprise that these books and essays are usually overcome with lament for America's lost youth, including much mourning about how the future will be far worse than our past, as we head over the hill as a nation. No wonder everybody's trying to hang on to their fast-fading salad years.

In contrast to these shopworn ideas, consider this mind-opening proposal from Stanford economist John Shoven. Writing in *Foreign Policy*, Shoven poses a simple question: Why not get rid of the old convention of measuring life from the beginning, which just plays into an overemphasis on obsolete markers like sixty or sixty-five? Instead, he suggests that we go the other way around and consider measuring life from the end. Using a mortality-risk model that is a much better predictor of true old age and infirmity, Shoven's analysis reveals that the proportion of those genuinely aged in society is growing only modestly, not nearly fast enough to warrant the worries so widely assumed. Shoven's message: "Our conception of what qualifies as 'old' has become old-fashioned."

He goes on to show the obsolescence of much that's accepted as hard reality by many economists and demographers today. When Social Security was enacted, Americans moving beyond sixty-five were considered "beyond the productive period," based on mortality risk. Just as we'd never consider equating 1935 dollars with 2010 dollars, should we expect 1935 ages to mean the same thing as those same indicators three-quarters of a century later? We need to longevity-adjust the meaning of ideas like the working-age population, just as we inflation-adjust currencies, in Shoven's compelling perspective.

Shoven's Stanford colleague, Center on Longevity founder Laura Carstensen, registers a companion point: All those years that have been added to life spans haven't simply been tacked onto the end. They have been contributed to the middle—mostly to the second half of life where health and capacity after fifty are being dramatically stretched.

These insights lead to a tantalizing conclusion: We're headed not toward the "aging society" as it is commonly conceived. We're instead witnessing an extraordinary explosion in the population between the middle years and late life. The big change under way might more accurately be described as the "new staging" of society—with the caveat that this development is part of an overall shift toward a greater proportion of the population on the older end of the age spectrum.

Our common misconception that soon a fifth or a quarter of the society will be "old" means that we're not able to recognize or understand the significance of a population explosion between midlife and old age, that we're failing to meet the needs and take advantage of the opportunities presented by this emerging group, and that we're overreacting to age-related challenges not nearly as burdensome as advertised.

BEYOND THE LONGEVITY PARADOX

Is it any surprise that the oxymoronic years—and all those chasms in identity and institutions and understanding—should lead inexorably to a longevity paradox? Put another way, how is it exactly that the best thing that ever happened to us as individuals, the extension of life and health to unprecedented ages, turns out to be the worst thing happening to us as a collective, that purported gray wave of greedy geezers about to take posterity to the cleaners? Should we disregard all that advice from our doctors about eating our vegetables, walking the stairs, and combatting stress if it's just going to produce mass misery in the end, flooding the world with millions of walkers crowding out all those strollers? And is that fate really inevitable? Is demography truly destiny? In his satirical novel *Boomsday*, Christopher Buckley offers a solution: euthanasia at seventy for boomers who want to leave the world better off for future generations. That's one way out.

While Buckley's treatment is tongue in cheek, others wonder out loud whether we're living too long for our own, and society's, good. Charles Mann, writing in the *Atlantic*, bemoans a "coming death shortage." Gregory Rodriguez of the *Los Angeles Times* asks, "Can we be too healthy and live too long?" decrying the social consequences of "large cohorts of the elderly, retired and healthy Floridizing all 50 states." Rodriguez sees an epidemic of loneliness, "a less optimistic and forward-thinking culture," a crime wave perpetrated by septuagenarians, and an overabundance of television shows romanticizing the 1960s.

But there is another way. We can break free from clinging to our lost youth, or for that matter, letting anyone stamp us as seniors before our time. We can accept the need for a new map of life that refuses to distort the territory opening up beyond the middle years. We can embrace this period and build off its unique assets. We can recognize that making the most of this period and the longevity bonus fueling it will take more than enterprising individuals with their DIY reinventions. In truth it will require a whole new set of social institutions, market innovations, enlightened policies, and a revised culture to go with them.

The great midlife migration is coming whether we like it or not. There's no going back to three-score-and-ten life spans. The difference is whether the intersecting demographic and longevity revolutions will mean calamity—or something quite the opposite, for individuals and society, for boomers and the generations to follow.

Here's a new mantra for this challenge: Sixty is not the new forty, fifty, or eighty—it's the new sixty. This group already arriving is neither old nor young nor some oxymoronic coupling of the two. They promise something new entirely. Facing up to this promise begins with shedding what author Matt Miller calls the tyranny of "dead ideas," those emissaries of cultural and social lag, notions and practices from the past that have outlived their usefulness yet assert themselves still.

And we'd better get going. This is not a fringe issue. We're not talking about a small segment of the population spending a few years off balance, muddling through. This group constitutes what may well be the largest group in society, entering a period that could approximate half their adult lives. In other words, as already argued, it may well be the biggest demographic development of the twenty-first century, one we're misunderstanding at vast peril.

A pair of fronts are beginning to meet, embodied in the two midlife crises described above: Millions of people are hitting a turning point in life, asking the big questions, thinking about what's next. They face a society that seems determined to shunt them into familiar categories even if they are ill-fitting traps. That indeed might produce the unhappy demographic storm some are predicting. However, if we seize the forces coming together, if we invent a new stage of life tailored to the contours and possibilities of this period, we might well produce a far more uplifting and powerful result, a fresh alignment to replace the world that's grown so out of whack.

Here's some good news: We already possess elements of a powerful vision for making the most of this opportunity. What's more, these ideas are almost entirely the product of revolutionary thinkers who themselves have arrived at this juncture in life, found the prevailing wisdom wanting, and set about crafting something better.

FOUR

New-Stage Thinking

....

In 1996, at the age of thirty-seven, I was awarded a midcareer fellowship. Never mind the suggestion that after a decade and a half on the job I was at the midcareer point. I probably qualified for a three-week vacation at best. But I was all too glad to take the opportunity to spend six months living in London, as a guest of the British government, having managed to live so far a thoroughly provincial life. It was a kind of gap year—at least half of one.

On the fiftieth anniversary of D-day, the UK decided to underwrite ten Americans a year to study a public policy issue of importance on both sides of the Atlantic. I proposed aging—which was an odd choice on the surface, since I'd spend my entire career to that point focused on kids growing up against the odds in the United States. But it wasn't such an odd choice under the surface. After ten years of working on ways to provide more mentors for young people in poverty, including a huge study of the impact of the Big Brothers and Big Sisters program, I was convinced that one of the best things we could do for young people facing difficult circumstances was to provide more opportunities for them to connect with adults who cared about them—mentors, youth workers, teachers, coaches.

At that time, 30,000 kids were languishing on the waiting list of Big Brothers and Big Sisters. I wondered where we'd find the human beings to do those things that only human beings can do, in large numbers and with the time to really connect. That question led inexorably to the vast, growing, and utterly underutilized human-capital bonanza that was older people. In that context, and working with others (including the late John Gardner), a group of us developed a kind of Peace Corps for the over-fifty population, aimed at bringing an infusion of caring and committed neighborhood adults into low-income elementary schools and into the lives of the children attending them. Called Experience Corps, it has since become one of the largest non-profit national service programs in America recruiting those in the second half of life. It currently serves 20,000 children, with extensive research showing Experience Corps produces powerful benefits for all involved—kids, schools, and Experience Corps members.

However, in 1995, when I headed off to London, Experience Corps was a promising idea awaiting seed funding, and I was at one of those rare moments in life when you can step back, take stock, potentially have some novel (even disruptive) experiences, and get ready for a new chapter. I had no family at that point, no mortgage, and an employer who (remarkably) promised to take me back when I returned.

During that time in the UK, given my espoused interest in the older population, I was stationed at two age-appropriate organizations: Age Concern, a leading advocacy organization, and the Institute of Gerontology at King's College, London. Both were established organizations with smart and committed people, only too happy to welcome a stranger into their midst. But the arrangement quickly got off to an inauspicious start.

On my very first day at Age Concern, housed in an impressive office block opposite London's Euston Station, I was so determined to impress my new colleagues that I stayed glued to my desk well past five o'clock. When I arose at eight in the evening, everyone else in my office had gone. In fact, everyone had gone. The building was completely shuttered. Doors bolted, lights out. After stumbling through dark corridors and stairwells for what seemed like hours, I finally found a door that opened. Bursting into the London night, I managed to set off a cacophony of flashing lights, wailing sirens, and clanging alarms—all the while summoning the City of London Fire Department. I had already achieved my goal of a disruptive experience—except that it was primarily disruptive for others. I should have known then that things were not going to unfold as planned, probably the first rule of any kind of sabbatical living and working in another culture, even one that seems on the surface as familiar as Britain.

The more substantive disruption would follow shortly, the result of discovering findings and recommendations from a recently completed report, "Inquiry into the Third Age," produced shortly before my arrival by the Carnegie Foundation in the UK. This "inquiry" was inspired by the ideas of an eminent Cambridge demographic historian named Peter Laslett, who argued that what was widely considered the aging of British society was really something different, the emergence of two distinct stages of life: the so-called Third Age and the Fourth Age. In Laslett's view, the two stages were being conflated at the peril of both groups.

Reading the Carnegie findings, and Peter Laslett's book that launched the ship, *A Fresh Map of Life*, I realized that I had come to the UK under confused pretenses. Experience Corps was targeting not the aged but the Third Age population, and the larger human resource opportunity I was so passionate about was intimately linked to the population that the Carnegie report was addressing—those between the middle years and old age. Looking back from the vantage of 2010, I now realize what I couldn't grasp at the time, that Laslett was proposing a solution to the oxymoronic years, the longevity paradox, and to much that ails us today.

THE PROPHECY OF PETER LASLETT

You might say that Peter Laslett saw it all coming. Looking across the sweep of four and a half centuries with a keenly honed historian's eye, Laslett concluded that we were in for a major shift. The combination of declining births and longer lives would not only produce a society with more people over the traditional retirement age but also force fundamental changes in the very nature and breakdown of the life course. Most notably, he predicted the emergence of a new life stage, which he chose to call the "Third Age."

For Laslett, this new map begins with the first age of dependence and childhood, includes a second stage of adulthood and midcareer jobs, and concludes with a final fourth age of dependency and ill health, the doorstep of demise. He argued that the difference in contemporary lives is the new territory emerging between the end of midcareer jobs and parenting duties and the beginning of dependent old age.

In redrawing the map of life, Laslett's immediate concern was to clear up a few fundamental mistakes. In his view, lumping everyone with gray hair under the same umbrella, and assuming this population in the future will look like and live like those of that age in the past, produced both a miscasting of reality and a miscarriage of justice. And it led to everything from damaged lives to bad policies. Laslett saw the conventional wisdom—that this population would be a vast burden to society, a huge drain on the medical establishment, an unproductive class inevitably focused on their own narrow needs—to be a result of "the persistence into our own time of perceptions belonging to the past." In other words, it was scenario planning through the rearview mirror.

By clarifying that the aging population is made up of a large group of people in the Third Age, and by a smaller group in the Fourth Age, Laslett hoped that we could better address the circumstances and needs of each group. While he was sympathetic to the plight of the Fourth Age population, and believed when push came to shove their urgent needs should always take priority over Third Agers' fulfillment, his primary goal was to elevate and illuminate the unprecedented opportunity he saw in the emergence of the Third Age in Britain and throughout the world.

A Fresh Map of Life, published in 1989, sets this all out. At its heart *A Fresh Map of Life* is a manifesto, if a particularly well-footnoted one, aimed at liberating the vast majority of those in their sixties, seventies, and beyond from the psychic strain of misclassification and from the very real consequences of being consigned to "mass indolence." Under the current arrangements, Laslett writes, "The waste of talent and experience is incalculable."

Laslett's anger is palpable, but so is his joy. He is as unflinching in embracing the possibilities of this period as he is in taking on those who dismiss them. In Laslett's telling, the Third Age isn't simply a better phase of life than commonly thought; it's the culmination, the "new crown of life," the "age of fulfillment." It's a time when individuals are liberated from the practical concerns and requirements of midlife yet years from old age. It's an opportunity for new pursuits, for learning and growth, for perhaps the most important contributions of one's life.

Laslett's core vision of the Third Age centers on responsibility. "Growing older does not absolve a person from responsibility, certainly not responsibility for the social future," he contends. "It could be claimed, in fact, that many more duties of older people go forward in time than is the case in those who are younger. This follows from the fact that they owe less to their own individual futures—now comparatively short—and more to the future of others—all others." As a result, Laslett writes, Third Agers must become "trustees for the future."

It's no surprise that given such an expansive, elevated, even romantic vision of this period, Laslett believed that the Third Age deserved its own standing, that it be more than young old age, or for that matter old middle age. Laslett picked the *Third Age* label based on the French phenomenon of lifelong learning academies called the Université du Troisième Age, which began flourishing during the 1970s and 1980s. The Third Age name, he believed, was not "tarnished" by the heavy stain of assumptions associated with old age.

In upholding the Third Age as a worthy destination in its own right, Laslett also sought to break away from the "cult of youth," a problem he believed to be prevalent in the UK and even more extreme in the United States, "a country so very anxious to be young." Doing so, he recognized, would require more than new thinking; it would take new arrangements. For Laslett, the Third Age revolution was dependent on "the development of an outlook, along with institutions and organizations, to give purpose to the additional years now being lavished upon us all." Laslett concludes with this prediction: "The emergence of the Third Age in the United States and the adoption of a fresh map of life will, I prophesy, be one of the most important of all social developments at the turn of the twentieth to the twenty-first century."

IN FRIENDLY SOLIDARITY

Not one to foist myself on Cambridge dons and other luminaries, I was sufficiently taken with Laslett's prophecy that I wrote him about what was under way in the United States to do just what he called for. I mailed the letter to Trinity College, Cambridge, Laslett's intellectual home, expecting to hear nothing in return. A week later I received an invitation to visit him at Cambridge.

As I waited in the entranceway of Trinity, on a bright May afternoon in 1996, amid the imposing grandeur of the centuries-old academic institution, my feeling was mostly unease. If there's a villain in Laslett's writing, it's well-intended Second Agers who think they know what's best for those in the next stage. The indictment rings throughout his book. I worried this might be a difficult encounter.

As Laslett bounded to the gate, a wiry bundle of evident warmth and vast enthusiasm, that image of the severe scold vanished immediately. He was eighty at the time, but without the slightest trace of infirmity; one colleague remarked that despite Laslett's great interest in the question of aging, the historian himself never seemed to age. He was carrying an edition of *A Fresh Map of Life*, inscribed to me, "In Friendly Solidarity." For the balance of the afternoon, I sat with him in Trinity's dining hall under portraits of Isaac Newton, Bertrand Russell, Ludwig Wittgenstein, and other distinguished alumni of the college. Laslett proudly noted that Trinity could claim more Nobel laureates than all of France.

What I came to realize that day and in later conversations is that just as Laslett saw the Third Age as a kind of culmination for society, the Third Age work was a personal culmination, drawing on all the strands of a remarkable career. The son of a Baptist minister of modest means, Laslett had come to Cambridge in 1935 and quickly established himself as a brilliant student. In World War II, which interrupted his academic career, he served in the Royal Navy, traveling dangerous supply routes through the icy waters between Britain and Russia. He barely survived. He told me that he'd been dubbed "Lucky Laslett" for managing to evade mortal harm during that period. He was eventually pulled from active duty and transferred to Bletchley Park, where he learned Japanese and became a code breaker in British naval intelligence.

After the war, Laslett diverted from the academic path again to work as a broadcaster and producer for BBC's Third Programme, the arts and culture channel that enabled him to pursue his lifelong interest in translating the world of ideas for a wide audience. He returned to Cambridge in 1948, eventually becoming a member of the History Department at Trinity College.

His accomplishments as a historian were prodigious. First, he revolutionized the history of political thought in Britain by discovering John Locke's library and using this somewhat serendipitous situation (Lucky Laslett . . .) to radically reinterpret Locke's writing. Soon he became more interested in how ordinary people conducted their lives than in the thoughts and lives and libraries of prominent figures. That pursuit led to crossing the boundaries of history and social science, employing new methods involving statistical analysis and technology and opening up the field of demographic history. His classic volume, *The World We Have Lost*, overturned long-accepted wisdom about the history of the family in Britain.

By the time he was in his fifties, Laslett had twice upended academic orthodoxy, in intellectual history and in social history, helping to create whole new schools of thought and approaches to scholarship. In the process he mentored a generation of leading historians in Britain, many of whom went into the field as a result of Laslett's spellbinding lectures.

Michael Young, a longtime Laslett coconspirator in various social reforms from the 1950s onward, recalls Laslett's lecture style. According to Young, "At the start of his lectures, Peter Laslett would take off his coat, take off his gown, take off his jacket, unbutton his shirt sleeves and roll them up, while the audience sat frozen in anticipation that, this time, he would take off all his clothes. Perhaps it was his wartime Japanese naval intelligence code breaking at Bletchley Park that gave him a taste for action."

Laslett and Young once hatched a plan as young lecturers to create a second university on the Cambridge grounds, accessible to ordinary people and designed to meet during the nearly half of the year when the regular Cambridge students were on break. Later they combined to cofound the Open University in 1969. Today, with 200,000 students, OU is the largest university in Britain and Europe and has long been a pioneer in distance learning and efforts to make education available to a much wider circle.

By the early 1980s, Laslett's growing interest in the transformation of the life course and in democratizing education led him to spearhead creation of the University of the Third Age in Cambridge—with Michael Young and a third scholar-entrepreneur, Eric Midwinter. U3A, as it came to be known, eventually grew to an enrollment of nearly a quarter million students, with all courses both taught and attended by individuals in the Third Age. He saw it as the first glimpse of the new kind of institution that would be needed to round out the Third Age—and in many ways the success of U3A as a venture in turn deepened and shaped Laslett's commitment to the Third Age concept.

By the time I got to know Laslett, he was dividing his days into three—mornings devoted to political philosophy, afternoons focused on demographic history, evenings dedicated to his work on the Third Age. That third area of work was the most deeply personal. It was something Laslett was quick to acknowledge. He emphasizes from the first words of the preface of *A Fresh Map of Life* that his perspective "belongs wholly to the later life of its author. My first writing on the history of ageing, and the earliest treatment of that subject, appeared when I was sixty-one and nearly all the rest of the work was done in my later sixties and earlier seventies. Here then is a report on experience as well as an exploratory analysis. It is itself a project of an individual Third Age."

Laslett died five years after we first met, in 2001, at the age of eighty-five, arguably in his Third Age until the last two weeks of life. The questions of justice between age groups and generations became a particular focus of those last years. In his final Third Age crusade, Laslett brought together his advocacy instinct, his gift for institution building, the communications skills he first honed at the BBC after the war, and his ability to envision and shape new paradigms. Using all those capacities, he became what might be characterized as a life-stage entrepreneur—unfortunately, one who did not live to see his work completed.

Although *A Fresh Map of Life* announces the emergence of the Third Age, it was really the possibility and the conditions Laslett unearthed and dissected that had emerged. After the appearance of the Carnegie Inquiry in 1992, Laslett pronounced optimistically, "The first and most important lap has already been run." More accurately, Laslett's pioneering vision probably constituted that first and most important lap—it certainly did for me, transforming the way I look at the Third Age and the life course more broadly.

Yet a quarter century later, what's abundantly clear is that life stages don't just emerge, and they take much more than that first lap, however important. They are by their very nature a long-distance quest—big projects requiring vision, language, leadership, institutions, and often social movements with multiple thinkers dissecting the same key questions. They also tend to take a long time. That's the way it's always been.

SOCIAL CONSTRUCTION PROJECTS

The impulse to divide up the life course in ways that tell a coherent story about the shape of a human life has deep roots. Shakespeare described seven chapters in *As You Like It,* beginning famously, "All the world's a stage, And all the men and women merely players; They have their exits and their entrances, And one man in his time plays many parts, His acts being seven ages." After reeling off the progression from Infant, to Schoolboy, to Lover, to Soldier, he crosses an age divide to Justice, Pantaloon, and the final, "Second Childishness": "Sans teeth, sans eyes, sans taste, sans everything."

Some scholars suggest that Shakespeare's seven ages are based on astrological divisions from as early as AD 90 that set "young manhood" at twenty-three to forty-one, "mature manhood" at forty-two to fifty-six, "old age" at fifty-seven to sixty-eight, and "decrepit age" from sixty-eight on up, or down, as the case may be. Athenian statesman Solon divided life into ten periods, somewhere around 600 BC, ending at the proverbial threescore and ten. At seventy, according to Solon, man "makes preparations for a not untimely death." Two centuries earlier Hippocrates provided his own division, concluding with "elderly," fifty to fifty-six, and "old" at fifty-seven. By the early fourteenth century, Dante offered a quartet of stages, concluding with *senettute* (old age) at forty-five to seventy and *senio* (senility) at seventy to eighty. The penchant by philosophers, poets, and other creative spirits to map and remap the life course reflects the essential truth that it is a creative enterprise, something we've been making up since the beginning of time and revising just as frequently.

And the process of invention is not confined to the written page. In the real world of society these stages are often mistaken for natural phenomena, as inevitable and undeniable as the rising and setting sun, the oxygen in the air. But in truth they too are fabricated. They're inventions, often spearheaded by life-stage entrepreneurs and visionaries like Peter Laslett. "Stages of life are artifacts," writes Harvard historian Jill Lepore. "Adolescence is a useful contrivance, midlife is a moving target, senior citizens are an interest group, and tweenhood is just plain made up." They're social construction projects, designed to solve a problem, take advantage of an opportunity, bring more sense into a world of chaos. What's more, they are under regular revision.

Writing in *Daedalus* in the 1970s, historian Tamara Hareven explains that American society began to recognize the presence of different stages of life in the latter part of the eighteenth century: "It discovered childhood in the first half of the nineteenth century and 'invented' adolescence toward the end of it, both emerging into public consciousness as a result of social crises associated with those age groups in a manner similar to the emergence of old age later on." She points out that in preindustrial society, "children were considered miniature adults . . . assuming adult roles in their early teens and entering adult life without a moratorium of their youth."

Hareven and other scholars suggest that the "discovery" of a new life stage is an extended and complex process that starts with recognition that this period is distinctive and discrete, that it has its own unique properties and integrity. Models who embody the period also help establish the new category. Addressing a particular need also helps create urgency and accelerate adoption, especially if members of the stage are linked to a social problem needing to be addressed. The last part is particularly key to instigating public policy.

My own research on the history of retirement in the United States led me to similar conclusions about the construction of life stages. While the economic institution of retirement grew steadily in the twentieth century, especially after the introduction of Social Security in the early 1940s, this time in life became seen as a problem period in the years after World War II. In the 1950s, for example, Lewis Mumford argued that at no point in society had any group been so rejected as older people were at that time.

But then it all changed. Beginning in the 1950s, we turned that stage of life from a dreaded desert to a cherished destination, transforming it into a cornerstone of the American Dream. A leisured retirement became a symbol of a life well lived, and whoever got there first was deemed all the more successful. In reality, that seemingly magical transformation was actually the result of a combination of interests that brilliantly fashioned this stage—marketers who sold the "golden years" ideal, financial-services companies that devised innovative ways for people to finance it, policy makers who created incentives for individuals to leave the workforce, and entire industries like the housing developers who built communities all over the country with names like Sun City and Leisure World, which not only helped people live out a dramatic version of this lifestyle but also served as symbols for the new dream. We built it, and they came, for decades on end.

Indeed, we seem to construct new stages of life every half century or so in this country, and prior to the mid-twentieth-century invention of retirement and with it the golden-years lifestyle, the most prominent American project in rewriting the map of life was adolescence.

THE INVENTION OF YOUTH

If Peter Laslett was the great prophet of the new and still largely unwritten stage being shaped between midlife and old age in the twenty-first century, Granville Stanley Hall was the preeminent figure in the invention of adolescence at the outset of the last century. Viewed from the twenty-first-century world of youth culture dominated by hip-hop and slackerdom, Hall seems an odd candidate to be the person bringing us what would eventually become the teenager. Born in 1844 into Puritan stock on a farm in western Massachusetts, he graduated from Williams College just after the Civil War. He was the class poet. After Williams he got a divinity degree, spent three years studying in Germany, and for a brief time was a parish minister. It quickly became clear that the clergy was not Hall's calling, and he returned to the academic world, first as a professor of English at Antioch College in Ohio before shifting to psychology.

It was a good move. Hall went on to become, arguably, the most important figure in the history of American psychology. In fact, his accomplishments were so seminal and so prodigious, it is hard to believe that they were all achieved by a single person. A graduate student of William James at Harvard, Hall received the first PhD in psychology in America; held the first chair in psychology in this country, at Johns Hopkins, where he also oversaw the first American psychology lab; and founded the American Psychological Association, as well as the *American Journal of Psychology*. Of the first fifty-four psychology PhDs in the United States, a full thirty were students of Hall's, and they included John Dewey, Arnold Gesell, and Lewis Terman. In 1889 he became the founding president of Clark University, a position he held for thirty-one years. In that capacity, in 1909, Hall brought Carl Jung and Sigmund Freud to Clark. It was, in fact, the only visit Freud ever made to this country; he hated the United States and returned home quickly. In a remarkable photograph from that visit, Hall sits, front and center, flanked by Freud, Jung, and Freud's biographer Ernest Jones. During the trip Freud, Jung, and William James all stayed at Hall's house.

In the 1880s and 1890s and beyond, Hall's study of the child did much to shape the field (which sought to understand the thoughts and feelings of children in fashioning their education and development) and the educational psychology field. However, at fifty he endured what could be called a full-fledged midlife crisis (remarkably, Hall may have been the first to actually use that term). His wife and daughter had died just a few years earlier from accidental asphyxiation. He complained of "the early psychic symptoms of old age" and struggled to make sense of years of research on the period beyond childhood. He felt lost, weary, and defeated.

Then he broke through, producing what would be his greatest work, the invention of a new stage of life between childhood and adulthood—which Hall would name "adolescence" in a 1904 landmark book of that title. As British cultural historian Jon Savage remarks, Hall's insight was to realize that "the intermediate state that Rousseau had both exalted and warned of was not just biologically determined but socially constructed." He adds, "Hall proposed nothing less than the creation of a new, generally recognized stage of life that would increase dependency and delay entry into the world of work."

In nineteenth-century America, boys became adults through entering the workforce or through marriage. If a child had the wherewithal to do adult work, he was an adult; if not, he remained a child. It was cut-and-dried. But by the latter part of the nineteenth century, conditions were lining up to create greater receptivity to the notion of an intermediate, protected period of development between childhood and adulthood. Industrialization, urbanization, immigration, and a growing fear of juvenile delinquency led to the sense of a growing and significant problem.

Hall thought of children as little savages whose hearts, bodies, and minds needed to be cultivated and carefully developed under the care of teachers, youth workers, psychologists, and other skilled practitioners. "Our urbanized hothouse life," he lamented, " . . . tends to ripen everything before its time." These notions found great receptivity among a wide array of thinkers and reformers and contributed to major changes, including the development of universal high school education and the spread of youth organizations like the YMCA, the Scouts, and Boys Clubs.

Hall published his two-volume thousand-page opus at age sixty, bringing together research he'd been conducting for years. Titled *Adolescence: Its Psychology and Its Relations to Physiology, Anthropology, Sociology, Sex, Crime, Religion, and Education*, the book played a catalytic role, providing various advocacy groups theoretical fortifications for their efforts to get young people off the streets and out of industrial workplaces and into classrooms.

Hall envisioned adolescence as a kind of waiting room between childhood and adulthood, a moratorium, one that liberated young people from the world of work and put them for a protracted period in an institution called high school. It was designed to be a safe place, a time for ripening. He likewise argued that high school should be extended to sixteen, which became enshrined in legislation that stands to this day.

Despite worries about juvenile delinquency and the perilous temptations of adolescence, Hall was actually a romantic about the possibilities of adolescence done right, wildly optimistic about its prospects. He writes in one passage, "Adolescence is a new birth, for the higher and more completely human traits are now born." This was not just an individual imperative, in his mind, but a national one. "In the present age of rapid transition and expansion," Hall writes, " ... [t]his is a good age to be young in." Elsewhere, he argues, "We are a nation in adolescence."

It took forty years to go from the introduction of the "adolescent" phrase to the emergence of the language of the teenager, the first appearance being a 1941 *Popular Science* article. However, it was the arrival in 1944 of the magazine *Seventeen* that marked the turning point from academic notion to pop culture. Just as the financial-services industry had played a critical role in the creation of golden-years retirement, consumerism and the need to sell products drove the teen identity. More than a half century later, the adolescent-turned-teenager remains a central part of the American landscape. In historian Thomas Hine's words, "It has become embedded in the way in which we imagine the shape of people's lives. It has become part of the cycle that begins at birth and ends at death. Nothing seems more real or more changeless than that."

LIFE'S INDIAN SUMMER

Given Hall's many achievements, it would have been no surprise if he regarded his retirement from Clark in 1920 at the age of seventy-six as a well-deserved rest after an extraordinary lifetime. Instead, two years later, and two years shy of his eightieth birthday and his own death, Hall published yet another opus, *Senescence: The Last Half of Life*. It is a remarkable document, a lost masterpiece. In it the person who gave us adolescence, who did so much to elevate the cult of youth, provides a vision for the new stage of life between midlife and old age—a kind of prophetic prequel to Laslett's articulation, yet more than a half century beforehand. Decades before anyone else, Hall recognized that longer lifespans, the exit from work, and narrowing family roles were opening up a gap in people's lives that had no meaning or purpose—and constituted a great loss to society.

Like Laslett's book, *Senescence*—with that title it's not hard to see why it was largely overlooked at the time of publication and remains obscure today—is in certain respects a scholarly work, written by a distinguished academic. Yet Laslett and Hall were both, in the end, social reformers, life-stage entrepreneurs, and advocates who had revolutionized disciplines and created new institutions. And they each articulated their vision of a new stage of life while inhabiting that stage, in books with deeply personal roots.

Hall begins *Senescence*, as Laslett starts his treatise on the Third Age, with his own version of a five-stage life course: "(1) childhood, (2) adolescence from puberty to full nubility, (3) middle life or the prime, when we are at the apex of our aggregate of powers, ranging from twenty-five or thirty to forty or forty-five and comprising thus the fifteen or twenty years now commonly called our best, (4) senescence, which begins in the early forties, or before in woman, and (5) senectitude, the post-climactieric or old age proper." He sees the penultimate stage growing not only in significance, but in duration: "We live longer and also begin to retire earlier, so that senescence is lengthening at both ends." It's worth noting that these words were written in the aftermath of *World War I*—decades before the first Social Security check, proclamation of longevity revolutions, or emergence of the concept of centenarians.

The year before *Senescence* was published, Hall wrote in the *Atlantic Monthly*, in singularly depressing fashion, that he was in a despairing state: "After well-nigh half a century of almost unbroken devotion to an exacting vocation, I lately retired. . . . Now I am divorced from my world." He went on: "I really want, and ought, to do something useful and with unitary purpose. But what, and how shall I find it?" One might think from these comments that *Senescence* is a book about being lost. It is, at times, despairing. But, overall, Hall presents an optimistic book that describes the new period as "an 'Indian summer,'" what he characterizes as "a precious bud of vast potentialities." Like Laslett, Hall calls on people in this stage of life to step forward to realize this potential, even as they are disregarded and dismissed, contending, "We have a function in the world that we have not yet risen to and which is of the utmost importance—far greater, in fact, in the present stage of the world than ever before."

In a reversal of his earlier theories, Hall argues that what society needs most is not youth but the qualities possessed by those in the second half of life: "Modern man was not meant to do his best work before forty but is by nature, and is becoming more and more so, an afternoon and evening worker," he writes. "Not only with many personal questions but with most of the harder and more complex problems that affect humanity we rarely come to anything like a masterly grip till the shadows begin to slant eastward, and for a season, which varies greatly with individuals, our powers increase as the shadows lengthen."

Although Hall never deals with it directly, his biographer Dorothy Ross points out that this view certainly reflects his own

trajectory—"the fact that his greatest creativity and accomplishment came after he reached the age of fifty." That experience may
well have shaped Hall's view that the assets of people who've had
adequate time to figure things out, who are good at synthesis, at
recognizing complex patterns, are needed more than ever: "Thus
as the world grows intricate and the stage of apprenticeship necessarily lengthens it becomes increasingly necessary to conserve
all those higher powers of man that culminate late." Hall sees
this period as a time characterized by putting one's experience
in service to others: "The fundamental passion . . . is to serve, to
subordinate self." And it is about service and altruism not just
in a general way but also in a generative way: "If he thinks of his
childhood and his forbears, he thinks still more of posterity . . .
to see the young better born and better provided for so as to
come to a fuller maturity."

Still, for all his enthusiasm about the value of this period, an
undercurrent of sadness runs through Hall's book. He asserts
energetically that for those in senescence, "The springtide of a
new stage of life stirs our pulses." However, there is recognition
throughout that this view is not shared by others in society:

> How little there is in common between what we feel
> about it and the way we find it regarded by our juniors;
> and how hard it is to conform to their expectations of us!
> They think we have glided into a peaceful harbor and
> have only to cast anchor and be at rest. We feel that we
> have made landfall on a new continent where we must
> not only disembark but explore and make new departures

and institutions and give a better interpretation to human life. Instead of descending toward a deep, dark valley we stand, in fact, before a delectable mountain, from the summit of which, if we can only reach it, we can view the world in a clearer light and in truer perspective.

In his view this disregard is a loss not just for those occupying the new stage but for a world that needs them, one that needs "those who are complete 'grown-ups,'" with "judgment about men, things, causes, and life generally that nothing in the world but years can bring." In the end, Hall is convinced that those in this stage must take matters into their own hands. "It is ours to complete the drama . . . to add a new story to the life of man," he writes, "We have too commonly accepted the conventional allotment of three-score-and-ten as applicable now."

NEW-STAGE SEQUELS

If Hall's vision amounts to a kind of *prequel* to Laslett's seminal articulation of what he calls the Third Age, then we have seen a steadily rising wave of *sequels* since the late 1980s, reaching a kind of critical mass in recent years. One strand in this new generation of thinking comes from leaders of the women's movement— including Betty Friedan, author of *The Feminine Mystique* and *The Fountain of Age*; movement icon Gloria Steinem, who wrote *Doing Sixty & Seventy*; and Suzanne Braun Levine, the founding editor of *Ms.* magazine. It should be little surprise that new-stage thinking would be coming from women moving into their sixties and seventies today; they are the same women who broke down gender barriers when they were starting out, in the 1960s and 1970s. They recognize the challenge of overcoming stereotypes and find themselves fighting once again for equal treatment and for the creation of new categories.

In *The Feminine Mystique*, first published in 1963, Friedan argues that "the problem that has no name—which is simply the fact that American women are kept from growing to their full human capacities—is taking a far greater toll on the physical and mental health of our country than any known disease." Third Agers, Friedan later wrote in *The Fountain of Age*, faced a similar situation without a shared identity or even a language to describe what they were facing.

In researching *The Fountain of Age*, published thirty years after *The Feminine Mystique*, Friedan made a pilgrimage to Peter Laslett, writing in the book about the possibilities of the Third Age and the need to fashion this new period. She also rails against the perils of "the youth short-circuit," a theme Gloria Steinem emphasizes in her 2006 book, *Doing Sixty & Seventy*. Steinem writes, "We've allowed a youth-centered culture to leave us so estranged from our future selves that, when asked about the years beyond fifty, sixty, or seventy . . . many people can see only a blank screen, or one on which they project disease and dependency. This incomplete social map makes the last third of life an unknown country." Steinem continues the metaphor: "More and more, I'm beginning to see that life after fifty or sixty is itself another country, as different as adolescence is from childhood, or as adulthood is from adolescence—and just as adventurous. . . . If it's to become a place of dignity and power, it will require a movement as big as any other."

Steinem then lays out the steps involved in transforming this new land into a place that people might actually look forward to reaching: "We may not yet have maps for this new country, but other movements can give us a compass," she writes. The social construction project starts by, "first, rising up from invisibility by declaring the existence of a group with shared experiences; then taking the power to name and define the group; then a long process of 'coming out' by individuals who identify with it; then inventing new words to describe previously unnamed experience." She goes on to underscore the importance of new policies and of then bringing this new view from the margins into the center.

Suzanne Braun Levine, who went from leading *Ms.* for almost two decades to authoring a series of thoughtful books about the new stage of life, reminds us that this is all anchored in a simple idea: "Fifty is the new fifty. Sixty, I hasten to add, is also the new sixty, and seventy the new seventy," noting that "the women who are the new fifty, sixty, and seventy wouldn't want to be anything else."

Two other visionaries have made some of the most significant contemporary contributions to advancing the new-stage mantle. One is Sara Lawrence-Lightfoot, a Harvard professor, MacArthur fellow, former board chair of the MacArthur Foundation, and one of the nation's preeminent experts on adolescence and public education. Lawrence-Lightfoot's writing about the importance of relationships in the development of young people had a profound impact on me when I was studying mentoring programs—and the imprint of her thinking very much influenced the creation of Experience Corps.

Although her professional work had largely focused elsewhere, Lawrence-Lightfoot—like Laslett and Hall, Friedan and Steinem—came to write about the new stage beyond midlife as she entered it herself. In 2009 she published a beautiful book, *The Third Chapter*, named for the period she defines as "the generative space that follows young adulthood and middle age." Lawrence-Lightfoot sees Erik Erikson's notion of generativity playing a central role in the emerging stage. Those who fail to be generative in this period—who fail to invest what they've learned from life in sustaining younger generations—are prone to stagnation and narcissism. They "often begin to indulge themselves as if they were their one and only child." In contrast, she describes the dynamic of "looking back" and "giving forward"— observing that often, "as we seek ways of giving forward to the next generation, we travel home to revisit the anchoring values into which we were socialized." Like Laslett, she argues that vision alone is inadequate, suggesting new rites of passage to help individuals make the developmental shift into the new period (even the equivalent to a bar mitzvah for entering the Third Chapter), along with a set of educational innovations that might better enable the transition to this period.

Anthropologist and writer Mary Catherine Bateson has also contributed mightily to illuminating the contours and possibilities of this emerging period. She likewise makes the case for why creation of this stage is critically important. The daughter of Margaret Mead and Gregory Bateson, she taught at Harvard, Amherst, and George Mason before leaving academia to focus on writing and activism.

In 2005 she authored a brief piece in the *Harvard Business Review*'s annual issue on the twenty-five big ideas for the year. In it, Bateson calls for establishing a midlife atrium—for building a break into our lives after fifty that in atrium-like fashion helps individuals let some light and air in, that provides space for exploration and renewal. These ideas draw on Bateson's belief that we've stretched midlife to the breaking point, that it has become like a run-on sentence, one in dire need of punctuation. Her words led us at Civic Ventures to try to find the right punctuation to break up that sentence. A period was clearly wrong; this juncture was not an ending. And a comma seemed inadequate. The semicolon, by contrast, captured the right sense of atrium-like renewal and redirection. Armed with the semicolon, we launched a branding campaign around the catchphrase "then; now" to help people realize that the transition period between midlife and the next chapter is a normal one. (I later wondered, after my own colonoscopy at age fifty, whether any play on the colon, especially a partial one, would have the right resonance with a boomer audience.)

In 2010 Bateson published *Composing a Further Life* (adapting the title of her earlier best-seller about the lives of five women). In it she eloquently sets out her theory of Adulthood II. Bateson defines the first stage of adulthood, Adulthood I, as the primary child-rearing and career-building period. Adulthood II follows, beginning as soon as forty for some, and extending past eighty for the most hearty. She describes the shift from Adulthood I to II as the time "when you reflect that you have done much of what you hoped to do in life but it is not too late to do something more or different," adding, "The doorway to this new stage of life is not filing for Social Security but thinking differently and continuing to learn."

For Bateson, a hallmark of the new stage is what she terms *active wisdom*. Wisdom is reaped from years of experience and living; she calls it the "most acceptable and positive trait associated with longevity." The *active* part describes the continuing "energy and commitment in the context of a new freedom" from the work and family constraints of the earlier stage of adulthood.

Life-stage visionaries like Lawrence-Lightfoot and Bateson are in good and growing company these days, as the ranks of new-stage thinkers become increasingly robust. Indeed, the flowering of ideas for what this period might look like continues apace, along with a feast of names for the phase. In addition to the Third Age and the Third Chapter, Second Adulthood and Adulthood II, Senescence and the Atrium, University of Minnesota sociologist Phyllis Moen, coauthor of *The Career Mystique*, has called the period "midcourse," while gerontologist Ken Dychtwald terms it "middlescence." Psychologist Laura Carstensen of Stanford describes an approximation of this period as Act IV (in a five-act life course) in her seminal book *A Long Bright Future*. Meanwhile, Tel Aviv University psychologist Carlo Strenger argues that we should have a "Life—Take2" in the second half of adulthood, contending that "thinking in two lifecycles should become a cultural norm."

In the UK, where the *Third Age* terminology remains in use, management expert Charles Handy writes, "The linguistic signposts are going up. The Third Age, the age of living . . . is already becoming a common term." Handy predicts: "There will soon be more talk of Third Age careers. Soon, no doubt, there will be Third Age societies and, ultimately, ministers for the Third Age in all OECD [Organisation for Economic Co-operation and Development] countries!"

Amid a growing body of names and ideas, key questions take on new importance: What in fact is the essence of this stage? What are its distinctive possibilities? What are we to make of the crescendo in new-stage thinking?

FIVE

The Next Map of Life

∙∙∙∙∙∙∙∙∙∙∙∙∙∙∙∙∙∙∙∙∙∙∙

My estimable mother-in-law, Donna Stone, has her own theories about this new stage of life. Sixty-three, with a younger sister who just turned sixty, Donna's life has been anything but lockstep. She was married right out of high school, had children early, and didn't go to college until years later—working as a waitress and typing dissertations at night to pay for tuition. Today she is the executive assistant to the dean of a university arts department, a new career she launched well into her fifties.

A few months back, I asked her what phase of life she is in. To my surprise, Donna told me that she and her sister debate this question a fair bit. They used to say late middle age—but how long can you be in "late" anything? Now when asked, she simply responds, "I'm on my next-to-last dog." The way Donna figures it, there are about five years left on her current dog, Jack, after which she could get another one, maybe a medium-size canine with an expectancy of ten to twelve years. It's not that

Donna expects she'll be getting measured for a casket at that point, but still she couldn't be confident about being around and physically able to take care of another dog for its full life span. She doesn't want to worry about orphaning the animal.

On a whim I went to the Web site of the foremost expert on centenarians, Thomas Perls, to do a longevity test on Donna—to see how many dogs she likely had left in her. After entering my best guesses about her circumstances, the site returned an estimated life span of ninety-seven. When I told Donna the good news, she went through the process herself. This time the program projected a mere ninety-six. "I know some things you don't," she quipped.

So maybe it's the last two dogs. We're used to measuring time in dog years, after all. This is just a variation on that familiar yardstick.

IT'S ABOUT TIME

"Last few dogs" probably won't catch on as a name for the new stage, especially given the already sizable list of contenders, among them Third Age, Third Act, Third Chapter, Second Adulthood, Adulthood II, Act IV, Midcourse, Middlescence, Late Middle Age, even Life—Take2. Senescence, anyone?

What's more, contemplating a label for this phase brings up prior questions about its essence. What is this period all about? What distinguishes it? What are the unique features that give it meaning and make it different from other periods in life?

Some of these attributes are recognizable, articulated by Peter Laslett and other visionaries who have called for establishing a new period between midlife and old age. We know this stage, at its most realized, can be a time of robust personal growth and *development*; it's likewise portrayed as an opportunity for continuing *contribution*—the chance to do some of one's most valuable work in a way that provides personal meaning and means something significant beyond ourselves. It also has a kind of *integrity*. Many who have written about the new stage emphasize that it needs to be seen as a distinct chapter in life, one with its own identity, coherence, and weight, a desired destination not some irksome chasm to be crossed.

Notions like development, contribution, and integrity help to home in on the key contours of the new stage but don't fully capture its core. Other stages of life are characterized by personal growth and development, important contributions, and a sense of identity and coherence. What is it exactly that makes the proposed new stage between midlife and old age distinctive and worthy of its own standing?

In my view, it all comes down to time—to three converging temporal dimensions that can be described as time lived, time left to live, and time beyond our lives. The intersection of these dimensions forms the heart of this period, helps explain why it matters for our own lives, and suggests how its creation might produce an extraordinary opportunity for society.

Time Lived

Time lived is the most obvious dimension of time associated with the new stage. It is more commonly known as experience. As someone who worked to create Experience Corps, I believe there

are real benefits to having been around the block. Indeed, at
Civic Ventures we talk a lot about the new demographics producing a potential "experience dividend," the payoff from tapping into the vast stores of human capital accumulating in so
many individuals in their fifties, sixties, seventies, and beyond.
That capital represents a huge investment by the country, and
by these individuals themselves, over many years.

Yet in our society the value of experience is often disregarded.
Seen as dead weight. Tossed away. "Finished at forty" is a slogan
that floats around Silicon Valley, near where I live. But I've seen
much that challenges this assumption. Take Gary Maxworthy.
Forty years ago, Maxworthy was an idealistic young man who
wanted to join the Peace Corps in the wake of JFK's call to service. But he already had a family to support. Instead of joining
up, he launched a career working in the food distribution business, where he ended up spending decades accumulating considerable expertise.

But as Maxworthy approached sixty, his wife was diagnosed
with terminal cancer. Her passing sent Maxworthy into a period
of soul-searching. As he stepped back and asked questions about
what matters most and what's next, he thought a lot about his
old Peace Corps dream and the prospect of returning to it. In
the end he settled for the more manageable domestic option,
VISTA, part of the AmeriCorps national service program. Based
on Maxworthy's substantial experience in the food business,
VISTA placed him at the San Francisco Food Bank. It was a
smart move. After Maxworthy had time to size things up, he essentially put two and two together. He discovered that the San

Francisco Food Bank—like food banks throughout the state of California—was primarily giving out canned and processed food. It was all they could reliably distribute without food spoiling.

At the same time, Maxworthy was aware from his previous experience that growers in California were discarding (and in the process wasting) an immense quantity of fresh fruit and vegetables each year because the products were blemished, not considered to be supermarket or restaurant quality. The only thing standing between two problems and a double win was someone with experience, know-how, and credibility who understood a better way of connecting supply and demand.

Enter Gary Maxworthy. Not only had he spent thirty years distributing food, he knew how to do so on a vast scale. Bringing this experience to bear on the food bank system, Maxworthy launched Farm to Family. In 2010 Farm to Family distributed more than 100 million pounds of fresh food to needy families in California.

Without question Maxworthy would have done a lot of good as a twenty-two-year-old Peace Corps volunteer, maybe taught reading or helped out in another worthwhile way, had he been able to get involved at that point. And that experience might well have shaped other life decisions along the way. But would he have been able to do something comparable to developing a system distributing 100 million pounds of food to hungry people— a year? That's the value of experience in a nutshell.

The experience-based, commonsense, problem-solving skills exemplified by Gary Maxworthy and his work are reflected in an accumulating body of research looking at the unique power of "grown-up" brains. This research shows that the two and two that Maxworthy so readily was able to put together, that ability to connect dots, is closely linked with acquiring an extensive body of experience over time.

Grown-up brains are good at connecting the dots because they see more dots. The contours of the situation, or as the case may be, the solution, are more evident as a result. It's a point made by science writer Barbara Strauch in her book *The Secret Life of the Grown-Up Brain*. Strauch shows that while certain kinds of deterioration in cognitive skills begin in our twenties, there are many ways that the brain actually gets better with experience. Although it might take brains of a certain age longer to assimilate certain kinds of fresh information, studies suggest they demonstrate a kind of "mental magic," in Strauch's words, to integrate information that's been incorporated over time. She explains that many experts "equate wisdom with an increased capacity, as we age, to recognize patterns and anticipate situations, to predict a likely future, and to act appropriately."

On the subject of acting appropriately, further research reveals how those with considerable experience tend to be less quick to judge than their younger peers. For example, a recent University of Michigan study shows that individuals at this juncture "make more use of higher-order reasoning schemes that emphasize the need for multiple perspectives, allow for compromise, and recognize the limits of knowledge." Those of a certain age, it seems, have an enhanced capacity to be flexible, accept uncertainty, and negotiate solutions. In other words, they are more mature. Eleanor Roosevelt got this point long before the social scientists could prove it with control groups and randomly assigned samples. "A mature person," she said, "is one who does not think only in absolutes, who is able to be objective even when deeply stirred emotionally, who has learned that there is both good and bad in all people and all things."

Time Left to Live

Whereas time lived, a.k.a. experience, is the most evident aspect of time as it relates to the new stage, an equally important and defining dimension of this period is the question of time left to live. Put simply, there is a growing sense of mortality that begins to dawn on people as they move through midlife. In my case it came about vividly when I hit my early fifties, faced a daunting health scare, and began a new family. At that time, I was acutely aware of a *simultaneous compression and expansion of time*— growing realization that our time here is finite, along with the simultaneous prospect of so much time ahead.

My generation and the ones just ahead of us are beginning to grapple with the essential truth that the road doesn't go on forever. At the same time, for those of us moving beyond fifty, there is an appreciation that it might go on for quite a while, for a period approximating the middle years in duration. That's something that—appropriately—dawns on few twenty-year-olds.

For some of us the trigger is the death of a parent, that emotional cushion that stands between ourselves and the realization of mortality. For others it is a health scare, a glance at the obituaries, that letter from AARP, hitting the big five-oh or even more likely six-oh, all reminding us that time is passing and thresholds are being crossed. The distinguished science writer Stephen Hall calls this shift in perspective "a kind of temporal continental divide." One of the first scholars to fully appreciate that divide was psychologist Paul Baltes. Baltes felt that as we traveled beyond midlife, "distance from death emerges as a stronger component of our time perspective." He explains, "As we deal with this change in our conception of 'lifetime,' as we count the years to live more than the years lived, the pressure to set priorities and to reevaluate the meaning of our lives increases."

Stanford's Laura Carstensen has taken this thinking to new heights, forging the time-based developmental theory she calls "socio-emotional selectivity." Through a series of landmark studies Carstensen shows that as individuals confront the finiteness and fragility of life, they focus more and more on what's important—and ignore those matters (and those people) deemed less so. This not only produces insight, and deepens relationships, but often results in greater happiness. Carstensen calls this the "positivity effect."

As Carstensen's work underscores, awareness of mortality can be unsettling, but it can also be rousing, pushing us from our day-to-day slumber to greater acceptance of the way things really are and the need to embrace what really counts.

For previous generations, the shift in perspective that comes with maturity likely arrived at a juncture when many were simply too worn out to do much with it. May as well kick back and get some much-needed R & R before it's time to meet the maker. You might say wisdom was wasted on the old.

Today a fifty-year-old man in the United States can expect to live past eighty, while a woman can count on living even longer.

And there's enough attention to the longevity revolution and enough evidence in our day-to-day lives of this change that we are beginning to internalize and accept the reality of the time ahead. It doesn't hurt to have former presidents like Jimmy Carter and Bill Clinton arguably doing their best work in a period beyond the supposed apex of midlife achievement—and for even as long a duration. Or to have financial-services companies reminding people how many "Happy 100th Birthday" cards were purchased in the preceding year.

The fundamental perspective produced by the expansion and compression of time is captured powerfully in the commencement address the late Apple founder Steve Jobs gave to Stanford undergraduates in 2005. In it Jobs—himself just past his fiftieth birthday—recounts reading a quote at seventeen that said if you live each day as if it were your last, someday you'll almost certainly be correct. According to Jobs, "It made an impression on me, and since then, for the past thirty-three years, I have looked in the mirror every morning and asked myself: 'If today were the last day of my life, would I want to do what I am about to do today?'" When the answer was no day after day, he knew it was time for a change. Remembering the finiteness of life became an invaluable way for Jobs to make big choices, "because almost everything—all external expectations, all pride, all fear of embarrassment or failure—these things just fall away in the face of death, leaving only what is truly important."

Then the inevitability of death took on more personal significance for Jobs. For all his money, confidence, brilliance, and seeming invincibility, Jobs was informed that he had pancreatic cancer that was almost certainly fatal, and in short order. He likely had three to six months to live: "My doctor advised me to go home and get my affairs in order, which is doctor's code for prepare to die. It means to try to tell your kids everything you thought you'd have the next ten years to tell them in just a few months. . . . It means to say your goodbyes." When the physicians later examined the biopsy of the cancer cells they extracted from his pancreas and discovered Jobs had an extremely rare form of the disease that is amenable to treatment, they wept.

Jobs understood mortality in a new way. As he explained to the Stanford graduates, "No one wants to die. Even people who want to go to heaven don't want to die to get there. And yet death is the destination we all share. No one has ever escaped it. And that is as it should be, because Death is very likely the single best invention of Life. It is Life's change agent." He concluded, "Your time is limited, so don't waste it living someone else's life."

Jobs was speaking to young people, about to start their lives and careers, but he might as well have been addressing his peers, moving through their fifties and sixties, beginning to understand emotionally that life has a beginning, middle, and end no one has ever eluded. Time matters at age sixty in a way that it doesn't when you are sitting at college commencement assuming an endless expanse ahead, even if some wise person is telling you otherwise. There's no more dress rehearsal. You're on.

In his book *Drive*, management expert Daniel Pink adds another critical element to understanding what motivates individuals at this juncture. Pink sees sixtieth birthdays as watershed moments for many boomers, a time when they begin grappling with questions of mortality while gaining a sense of possibility in the new profusion of time ahead. Then Pink adds a third and critically important component to this equation. He posits that there is some relief in realizing at sixty that you're likely to have another twenty-five years to do those things that matter most. A sense of relief . . . until you remember how fast the last twenty-five years shot by. Pink believes that this realization will produce a boomer-led elevation of purpose, which he defines as "a cause greater and more enduring" than oneself. As Pink predicts, "When the cold front of demographics meets the warm front of unrealized dreams, the result will be a thunderstorm of purpose the likes of which the world has never seen."

Time Beyond

Groucho Marx famously remarked, "Why should I care about posterity? What's posterity ever done for me?" The late American historian Christopher Lasch offers a response. The prospect that we live on in future generations is what "reconciles us to our own supersession" and helps us come to terms with "the central sorrow" that we will eventually grow older and die, a notion in Lasch's mind "more harrowing even than frailty and loneliness."

Just as the compression of time gets us going, helping us focus on the most important things, and reminds us that the time to act is now, it brings with it the inescapable realization that no matter how well we do on the longevity index, we are linked to a future extending beyond our lives, one that we will never actually see. As already noted, psychologist Erik Erikson inelegantly called this impulse "generativity." *Generativity* is right up there with *senescence* in the phrase-making pantheon. It's anything but inspiring. But the concept behind it is profound. It's a reminder that there is direction to the potential thunderstorm of new-stage purpose, and that natural direction is the well-being of future generations.

Erikson explains that the hallmark of successful development can be encapsulated in the phrase, "I am what survives of me." Adults who have moved beyond the pull of stagnation and narcissism are able to focus on nurturing the future, on caring and responsibility that extends from one generation to the next generation, that "outlives the self," in the phrasing of writer John Kotre. Indeed, for Erikson generativity is the place where the cycle of life and the cycle of generations come together.

Generativity can be expressed in many ways. Parenting is the most obvious form. Teaching, mentoring, coaching, and other vehicles all aimed to connect to posterity are other examples. Whatever the particular manifestation, Northwestern University scholars Dan McAdams and Regina Logan explain the essential power behind the concept: "The narrative beauty of generativity," they write, "is that it provides a way of thinking about the end of one's life that suggests that the end is not really the end. I may die, but my children will live on. My own story may end, but other stories will follow mine, due in part to my own generative efforts."

One of my favorite examples of generativity in action is Gene Jones, a former World War II bomber pilot who made a living turning around businesses. At the age of eighty-four, he decided to create Opening Minds Through the Arts in the Tucson, Arizona, public schools, based on the multiple intelligence theories of Howard Gardner and in response to what he felt were unfortunate arts cutbacks in public education. Today the program serves more than 20,000 children, and Jones is actively involved in his midnineties. As Jones's story suggests, while generativity is expressed in various ways across the life course, the post-midlife period represents something of a high-water mark for the impulse, most likely triggered by the question of mortality.

Susan Krauss Whitbourne, a psychologist at the University of Massachusetts, for example, conducted a longitudinal study over three decades looking at adult development. In her research, Whitbourne found that participants who scored high on self-fulfillment in the middle years and beyond were engaged in work that moved them beyond narrow personal concerns to concern for others. She finds particularly that "the desire to leave a positive legacy is a fundamental motivation that in turn serves as the ultimate basis for self-fulfillment."

Perhaps what is most unique about generativity in the new stage—in contrast with the past—is that the concept of the compression and expansion of time allows individuals not just to leave a positive legacy, as Whitbourne underscores, but to actually invest their time in work that will make the world a better place for future generations.

In the past when people hit their sixties or seventies, the default legacy option was to donate money that might do some good after they were gone. Now more and more individuals have the opportunity to *live a legacy*—not just to leave one.

Come Together

In contemplating the essence of the new stage, I'm reminded of the motto of the French Revolution: *Liberté, Egalité, Fraternité*. When the new stagers storm the barricades of change, perhaps they will be chanting their own tripartite anthem inspired by the intersecting dimensions so influential in shaping this period: Mortality, Longevity, Urgency. Or, even better, Mortality, Longevity, Generativity. Whatever the mix, it is no wonder Peter Laslett was so optimistic about this period and its prospects. To him, the "crown of life" had shifted from the middle years to this emerging period. When I first read that assertion it seemed like overreaching to me. I'm an admitted enthusiast about this phase and its possibilities, much as Laslett was. But the new crown of life?

After years of conducting interviews and thinking about this prospect, I now have greater appreciation for Laslett's perspective. Of course, every stage of life has its high points and unique attributes. However, the period opening up in the bonus decades beyond midlife marks an extraordinary coming together of experience, perspective, motivation, capacity, and the time do something with it all. Or, put differently, it's a time when many have insight about what matters, a special impetus to act on this wisdom, and the ability to do so. In this respect, it's a potential sweet spot, a confluence rather than a reinvention.

Or for that matter an oxymoron. Rather than the incongruity of being young old, a split difference, half of one recognized category and part of another, the new stage has the prospect of becoming a new kind of integration, connecting past and present, intellect and emotions, in a way that's uniquely powerful. That's what Mary Catherine Bateson means when she talks about "active wisdom" or Laura Carstensen suggests when she describes a time when individuals "think with their hearts and minds simultaneously."

As Laslett alerted us, for all these reasons the new stage has the potential to be *the* destination, what we've been working toward. If we fully realize this potential, it is a stage that people will strive to get to as quickly as possible, much in the way an earlier generation rushed to *early* retirement. Once there, they'll very likely endeavor to stay as long as possible.

THE NEXT MAP OF LIFE

A century ago G. Stanley Hall called for a new narrative to be written, completing the tale of life's stages, one he felt lacked a full plot. What's needed, he said, was more than an edit of the existing life course but a new drama that builds at a different pace and reaches its high point in the years when decline was once thought to be the natural order of things. Hall set out five stages. There's a case to be made for a Shakespearean seven, although configured differently (and without childishness repeated at the end). These stages include childhood (roughly birth to ten), adolescence (ten to twenty), emerging adulthood (twenty to thirty, another new stage, emerging over the past decade), middle age (thirty to fifty-five or sixty), *the new stage* (fifty-five or sixty to eighty), retirement, and true old age (together from about eighty onward).

The Bard aside, I'm attracted to the simplicity of Laslett's quartet. A first stage of roughly birth to thirty, comprised of childhood, adolescence, and emerging adulthood; a second period encompassing the middle years, focused on establishing careers, forging families, and the other tasks of midlife, stretching to fifty-five or sixty; the new stage that Laslett called the Third Age, beginning where the middle years leave off and lasting until eighty; and the final stage of retirement and old age, most likely and ideally significantly shorter in duration than the preceding periods.

It's always treacherous assigning ages to stages, and these years should be seen as the roughest approximations. That's certainly true with the new stage. To be sure, some will get there in their early fifties, maybe even earlier (Meredith McKenzie is one example), and many will remain in this stage beyond the big eight-oh (as Gene Jones's tale reminds us). In my experience the fifties are frequently the on-ramp to the emerging stage, a time of consideration, exploration, and reflection, focused on what's next, and the eighties a time when many shift to a new life mix.

Whatever its chronological beginning and end, the new stage between midlife and old age is distinctly not defined by the traditional markers of retirement, the end of work, and the end of family duties. Economic necessity and psychic significance, for example, are making work a centerpiece of these years. It is also worth acknowledging flux: The life course is a dynamic and ever-changing enterprise, one that raises further the question of what we should call this period soon to be occupied by all those fifty-, sixty-, and seventysomethings.

I found myself thinking about this challenge recently, while looking at a collection of greeting cards in a museum shop, birthday notes clearly aimed at this demographic group. The first one proclaimed proudly, in bold and attractive lettering: "Of a Certain Age," followed by "The Big Five Oh!," "60 ISH," "70 ISH," and "80 ISH." Then the optimistic, "Aged to Perfection." The last—my favorite—read "Extremely Late 30's." So perhaps "Extremely Late 30's" joins "Next-to-Last Dog" as the latest candidate for naming the new stage between midlife and old age.

Or maybe not. In contemplating names, I'm drawn to Hall's notion of this period as something higher, a vista from which one can make out patterns, understand complexity, and more clearly appreciate what's most important. A kind of higher adulthood. There's something to be said for mature adulthood, as well, in capturing a time when individuals have achieved the qualities of balance and discernment Eleanor Roosevelt ascribes to maturity, although the echo of "modern maturity" and other musty uses of that word cut into its appeal.

If we opted for a single word, *confluence* beautifully captures the integration at the heart of much that is attractive about this period. The dictionary describes *confluence* as "a flowing together of two or more streams," a "coming together of people or things." That sounds right to me. And it reminds me of visiting Confluence Park with Meredith McKenzie, whose own life embodies this kind of coming together to reach a new and higher purpose.

Some I've talked to suggest, simply, the *New Stage*, in part because it describes the next frontier on the life course and equally because it distinguishes this period from anything resembling old age. One could argue, with merit, that this condemns the label to temporary status, a placeholder. Then again the New School in New York was founded in the aftermath of World War I, while New College, Oxford, was established in 1379 . . . and is moving toward its 650th anniversary.

But to my mind, the Encore Stage—or Encore Adulthood—is the answer, best capturing the new phase that is opening up between the middle years and late life. It locates its place in the new map of life, parallels emerging adulthood on the other side of midlife, and gives the new phase appropriate standing and weight as one of life's major periods.

So for now, and for the purposes of this book: the *Encore Stage*. Its denizens, "Encore Adults"—or how about simply "grown-ups"?

REALIZING THE POSSIBILITIES

Consider the prospect of tens of millions with experience, perspective, and capacity, and one begins to glimpse an emerging sweet spot not just for individuals but for society as well, a nation of grown-ups uniquely suited to taking on the complex challenges of our time. As uplifting as this prospect is, there is no escaping the need for realism when it comes to realizing these possibilities. I'm reminded of historian Thomas Hine's comment about G. Stanley Hall's enthusiasm for adolescence. Hine points out that from reading Hall, one might have assumed adolescence was lived out in Valhalla, when in reality it occurred in a place called high school.

Indeed, just as everybody who gets older doesn't get wiser, not everyone will find the ideal I've upheld in the preceding sections or that is suggested by some of the labels above. Many will face health issues—their own and those of family members—that will impede their ability to act on this unique combination of factors. Many will simply not have the wherewithal—financial, emotional, logistical—to make critical changes in their lives. Longevity itself is deeply linked to education and class. There are differences in the experiences and prospects of women and men as they approach this phase. And there are ways that this new stage could backfire, contributing new rigidities to another lockstep life course rather than opening up more opportunities for development, contribution, and meaning.

Our ability to make the most of the possibilities presented by a new stage of life will require facing up to these and other formidable challenges. In doing so we likewise need to remember that we're not just carving out a new period for those who will inhabit it now, or even in the future. We're remaking the entire shape of lives. This stage will change the nature of every other stage and have an impact that resonates throughout the life course. That's why it is not just up to us at the vanguard of this new period to be involved in creating a new stage of life; it's a project for all ages. The whole of society has a stake in the outcome.

The time for that project has come. A perfect storm of circumstances—yet another confluence—is lining up behind this project: the demographic revolution of nearly 80 million boomers moving through their fifties, sixties, and soon seventies; the longevity transformation that is extending life spans throughout the developed world; economic circumstances that are pushing toward longer productive (and income-earning) lives, along with policy changes that seem to be heading in the same direction; a raft of research showing the vast capacities of people in the second half of their lives, far beyond what was long assumed; and even negative forces, such as all the worries that an increase in the proportion of individuals over sixty is going to cause serious problems. This kind of concern, in the past, has often served as a powerful force in the creation of new stages.

These potent conditions join powerful vision to help push us toward a decision—one that would create this stage as a route to bringing more sense to individual lives and society more broadly, to turn what is widely portrayed as a kind of national midlife crisis into America's midlife opportunity. The midlife migration is on its way. Whether "we build it" or not, they will come. What happens will depend on how adept we are at designing this new period and the culture, institutions, and other features that go with it.

There are signs of organizational creativity and change already under way, of new pathways, programs, and policies, inklings of a landscape better aligned to a twenty-first-century life course. It's no surprise that many of the most innovative are taking form in the transitional space from the middle years to the new chapter, as so many are lining up to cross into this new land.

SIX

Routes of Passage

·····················

Standing confidently in front of her blue-uniformed fourth graders at the Cole Arts and Science Academy, a publicly funded charter school in Denver, Paula Lopez Crespin is not what she seems. Crespin appears to be a veteran teacher, someone who has been in the classroom for twenty or thirty years. In fact, she's a Teach for America (TFA) recruit, a brand-new educator learning on her feet in an intensive immersion program designed to help the best and the brightest become teachers.

She is not your typical Teach for America recruit, either. TFA has a reputation for attracting high-flying twenty-two-year-olds from the best public and private universities in the country. It's such a coveted placement that 12 percent of all seniors at Ivy League schools applied in 2010. Of the more than 46,000 applications, only 12 percent were accepted. And of those, according to a TFA news release, only 14 percent "are professionals who completed several years of full-time work before applying to Teach for America." The vast majority are right out of school.

From a blue-collar family, the fiftysomething Crespin initially went to nursing school, but at nineteen decided it wasn't for her. She headed into the job market instead, landing an entry-level position as a teller at a local credit union, attending community college at night, and steadily working her way up the ladder of the organization. Eventually, she got a business degree, at thirty-seven, and became a marketing vice president.

Over time, Crespin developed qualms about the credit union's practices and management. She also felt a growing pull toward the education field, having admired several relatives who became teachers. It still took years to go from her credit union career to one in education. At the time, her daughter was in high school, her son was in grade school, and the credit union salary was better than she could get starting out in the classroom. She reflects, "It wasn't something I was able to do financially right away. Every year I had growing dissatisfaction with my job, but there were pay increases all the time. It was not an easy decision to say I'm not going to do this anymore."

Crespin's departure, protracted as it was, turned out to be a smart decision. The unease she felt about the credit union was confirmed when it was taken over by a regulatory agency, which ousted both the board and the leadership. En route to her new path, Crespin took time out to help her husband recuperate from surgery—while investigating alternative licensing programs for people outside of education who wanted to become teachers. She found these offerings confusing and chaotic. She even questioned her desire to go into the education field. However, during this period she was exposed to substitute teaching, which she loved, even if the $100-a-day salary wasn't enough to live on.

Given the financial realities, Crespin was soon back in the credit union field, working for another organization. She felt like she was heading backward. Then came a turning point. Crespin's daughter graduated from the University of Colorado and was accepted into Teach for America. Ironically, Crespin initially resisted the TFA route for her daughter, worried for her safety as a young female teaching in a tough neighborhood.

When she visited her daughter's Los Angeles classroom, it was transformative. "I was sitting in the back and wanted to wave to her, but she was in a zone, in command," Crespin recalls. "She was the best teacher I had ever seen."

In a turnaround of the old pattern, Crespin followed in her daughter's footsteps—applying for Teach for America despite its image as a pathway for high-achieving recent grads, all with her daughter's help and her staunch support ("She's just a great cheerleader").

It quickly became clear that beyond the high hurdle of getting accepted into the program, making it in TFA was an equally formidable task. Crespin wondered if she would have the energy: "The more they told me about the commitment, the more I realized this was going to be a very tough assignment."

Soon Crespin was at TFA's institute for new recruits, living for six weeks in a sweltering dorm in the summer Houston heat, fitting into the cramped, utilitarian space with three twenty-somethings fresh from college and sharing a bathroom down the hall. It was a far cry from the adult life she'd lived for decades. "Honestly," she states, "to live in a dorm room at this age is no picnic. . . . It was like boot camp. You're in the trenches. You're in these lousy accommodations. You're doing tons of work—lesson planning, classes at night. You get up at 6:00 in the morning, you have breakfast, you get on a bus and go teach summer school for an entire school day. You come home and eat. You do more lesson planning. And you have class at night. A lot of times I didn't go to bed until 2:00 a.m. . . . Then you get up again at 6:00 a.m."

Crespin wasn't even the senior member of her training group—one colleague was a sixty-two-year-old former employee of the phone company. They both made it through. And the experience wasn't just an endurance test. "When I think about my brain before I went into the program and my brain after the program, so much knowledge was imparted," she says, acknowledging that she was stunned both by what she learned and by her capacity to learn it.

Crespin now routinely works sixty-hour weeks, sharing a class with a twenty-three-year-old fellow TFA recruit, teaching math and science to third and fourth graders. She's used to working long hours from her previous jobs and parenting duties, so that hasn't been as big an adjustment as it might have been for some. The whole process has presented economic challenges. Her husband has also gone through a career change, including a master's in social work. The lower salary plus tuition bills have meant sacrifices—they haven't moved into a three-hundred-square-foot garage like Meredith McKenzie, but they've refinanced, tapped into retirement savings, and changed their entire lifestyle and spending patterns.

According to Crespin, so far it's working out. She loves teaching and she loves TFA: "If I were ever to consider stopping working in the classroom, it would probably be to work for TFA, the organization." Perhaps most important, she's in a school that "wants teachers that make a difference, teachers that want to work late," who are committed to the kids. She admits considerable stress trying to reach young people in the short time she has with them, particularly the critical third-grade year. There are plenty of obstacles: "What concerns me the most is that they have these issues at home that I can't even imagine. If that's going to be so consuming, is all the work we do in the classroom going to mean anything in the long run?"

Still, Crespin believes this is her moment to try. "When I was thirty-five and really at the peak of when my own kids needed me most, I don't think I could have done it," she says, "not in the same way I can do it now. I'm in the right place in my life. I'm an empty nester. My daughter's married. My son is in college, and my husband's a social worker. We both work a lot of hours, and we both like our jobs. I don't cook like I used to. My house isn't spotlessly clean like it used to be. But I can do this kind of work right now."

FROM THEN TO NOW

Paula Lopez Crespin's story of finding her way through a passage aimed at younger people echoes the odyssey of John Kerr, living in the state of Wyoming, near the northeastern corner of Yellowstone National Park. Wyoming is a long way from where Kerr spent most of his life, working for forty years at Boston's

main public television station. He arrived at WGBH straight out
of college in the 1960s, after landing an internship there.

Nudged out the door at sixty-five, divorced with three adult
children, Kerr determined to get out of town. The on-air face of
station fund-raisers for decades, he'd had it with being accosted
at the supermarket by people who recognized him as the pledge-
drive pitchman. He stuffed his possessions into a storage locker,
sold his house, and headed for Wyoming, a place he'd frequented
on vacations over the years. Sounds like the tune-up for a classic
retirement story, the outdoorsy version. But Kerr wasn't heading
in that direction. His goal was to work in the national parks.
Here he (like Crespin) was heartily encouraged by his daughter,
Rosi, a forestry school graduate and founding executive director
of Gray Is Green, a group designed to encourage green retirement communities. It was another case of a parent following in
an offspring's footsteps.

How did Kerr go through his transformation from midlife to
a new stage, from a fund-raiser to someone working on environmental issues three-quarters of the way across the United
States? He went back to a familiar formula—he did an internship, the same kind of route that worked when he was at the start
of his career. Kerr joined the Student Conservation Association
internship program, where he spent a period of months shifting
through a group designed for people just like him—well, just
like him, but almost a half century younger. Everyone else was
about nineteen.

Today, Kerr is a summertime park ranger in Yellowstone, with
the job of keeping people and bears away from each other. Dealing with the government bureaucracy has brought frustrations,

but he proudly has "one of those ranger hats" and a badge to boot, and he draws on newly acquired EMT skills in the conduct of his job. In the off-season he is plotting to develop an initiative that would enable people over fifty to more easily find work in the national park system.

Paula Lopez Crespin and John Kerr are part of the great midlife migration, as they wend their way into uncharted territory toward the new stage of life. Without clearly defined and well-established rites and routes of passage, it's as if they are sneaking in the side way, contorting and distorting themselves to use the pathways and resources readily available for a life and work transition but designed for a target audience about half their age. Crespin and Kerr are in the midst of the do-it-yourself shift. As many transitioning in their fifties, sixties, and seventies have sadly discovered, do-it-yourself, a kind of individual improvisation, is oftentimes all there is.

Where are the *rites of passage*, the counterpart to the gold watch or the retirement party, or for that matter the high school or college graduation (or even, as Sara Lawrence-Lightfoot suggests, the equivalent to the bar mitzvah) for those entering the new stage? Just as important, where are the *routes of passage*, the pathways and institutions that can ease the process and move it from a DIY challenge faced by one person at a time to something more reliable and sturdy for millions of people at once?

The need is vast, it demands new arrangements, and it starts with what authors Carlo Strenger and Arie Ruttenberg call "the existential necessity of midlife change." The much-vaunted midlife crisis is more accurately the vast challenge of midlife transition—really, postmidlife transition—no simple matter under any circumstances. My colleague Bill Pace, who initially trained as a teacher but then spent a full career in other pursuits, has spent several years navigating back to his earlier aspiration—taking his midlife experience with him as part of the package. When I asked him about the process, Pace's counsel was simple but telling: "It's a transition, not a transaction," he states. Pace describes a shift that is rarely an overnight accomplishment or a magical reinvention. It is about integrating a variety of strands and skills, present and past. It is as much about *who* you'll be as *what* you'll do or *where* you'll work, although the shift usually involves all these dimensions. It's a change in various proportions personal and professional, financial and developmental. It's the movement from one stage of life to the next.

Bill Pace's insights fit the perspective of William Bridges, one of the wisest observers of life change and author of the book *Transitions*. Bridges studied an array of transitions, from divorce to layoffs and much in between, concluding that almost all seem to follow three sequential phases. The first is "Endings," with all its mourning and sense of loss; the middle is what Bridges calls "The Neutral Zone," a time of identity confusion and other dislocation; and the third phase he calls "New Beginnings," when the gap that's formed is filled by new relationships, structure, and purpose.

Although a certain amount of opportunism, pluck, and luck will always be part of life transitions, easing the transition process calls for more pathways, organizations, and other institutional arrangements designed to help make the most of the emerging years after midlife, especially given the vast numbers of boomers and others who are coming down that road. As

Daniel Boorstin observed, we haven't done nearly so well in this sphere as we have in developing comparable pathways and institutions aimed at younger people.

That said, fresh arrangements are beginning to take shape, pointing the way to expediting this shift and making it less exclusively a solo journey of improvisation. The appearance of this new generation of institutions parallels the rise of new-stage thinkers and a vanguard of role models living out a vision of life and work in this new period before it even has an established name. And it is probably no surprise that many of these innovations have started in many of the same commonsense areas developed to help young people make the shift to adulthood—advice and counseling, higher education, and experiential opportunities like internships and service. (It is also no surprise, in the current economy, that these transition vehicles are commonly focused on a new stage of work as well as life, oftentimes an encore career at the intersection of money, meaning, and impact.) Overall, it seems that these time-tested approaches to transition support are just as valuable at sixty as at twenty.

Before exploring a broader set of ideas that might contribute to what's needed, it's worth looking more closely at several of these transition-focused innovations, some adaptations of existing pathways and some entirely new routes. They provide a flavor of the ferment under way—and a hint of the foment yet to come.

A NETWORK OF ONE'S OWN

After twenty-six years in the for-profit sector, first as a lawyer and then managing corporate projects, Betsy Werley was ready

for a change. She wanted two things in a new life: meaning—
"You know that old word, *meaning*?" she says—and a leadership
role that allowed her not just to recommend change or write
memos about change but to actually make change.

As Werley started to network, talking to friends and friends
of friends about nonprofit jobs, she met with a highly respected
"guru" in the not-for-profit world, a man who has been a top executive in both government and nonprofits. "He looked at my
résumé," Werley recounts, and "he said, 'You've got really terrific
credentials, but you don't really fit into any specific nonprofit
job. You're not a marketing person; you're not a development
person; you're not a programming person; you're not a financial
person. Nevertheless, a nonprofit would be lucky to have you.'"

Nice backhanded compliment, Werley thought, but not exactly helpful advice. She kept talking to people until eventually
she heard about an executive director job at a relatively new nonprofit called the Transition Network, a volunteer-based organization for women over fifty who want to support, help, and
advise one another as they move together into a new stage in
their lives. The Transition Network was launched in 2000 by
new-stage social entrepreneurs Charlotte Frank and Christine
Millen, two veterans of the women's movement, united in their
confusion about what to do next in their own lives. "Out of our
puzzlement," Frank says, "we realized that we needed to do what
we always did in the past when we faced similar quandaries. We
needed to talk to other women." What began with Frank and
Millen's mutual support grew rapidly.

Soon the New York City chapter of the Transition Network
had grown to a thousand women and had to be capped, like one

of those mutual funds you can't get into anymore. Media attention on the network led to requests from women in cities around the country. And Frank and Millen realized they needed a full-time executive director. "The year before, the organization's total budget was $40,000," Werley recalls. "I had moments when I thought, 'I really think they're on to something, but am I really going to do this?' And then what convinced me was that every woman over the age of forty, when I talked a bit about the Transition Network, would say, 'Take the job and call me, because I need this organization!'"

Since then, the group has grown as much as 30 percent each year and now involves 2,500 members in a dozen chapters across the United States. Its members are government workers and artisans, nurses and journalists, accountants and academics, many concluding careers that would have been off-limits to their mothers' generation, turning to each other for support as they once again enter choppy waters.

The organization is built on two types of peer groups. Transition peer groups, typically eight to ten members, help women "who want to articulate, define, think through, and manage change in their lives." Explicitly "not therapy groups," the transition groups focus on new-stage issues, such as use of time, new identity, separation from professional colleagues, making new friends, risk taking, and the like. The second type of group focuses on topics of strong interest to members, such as women's entrepreneurship and the use of technology. These smaller sessions are supplemented by monthly chapter meetings featuring talks on subjects including employment options, finances, wellness, and encore careers.

The Transition Network also offers the Caring Collaborative, essentially a support group and service corps in which members provide short-term services to help other members remain independent when they hit a health crisis, from breaking a leg to cancer. And Transition Network members gather to provide volunteer service for the community by using their experience— no stuffing envelopes. In effect, the Transition Network is a vibrant new-stage service lodge for women over fifty, one focused on life and career transitions, subsisting on dues, and anchored in communities where its chapters reside.

The Transition Network provides help organized along gender lines, but there is an upsurge of new transitional groups and other support arrangements organized in all kinds of ways. It's becoming common for colleges and universities to provide career services to encore phase alums; Northwestern, for example, in 2009 provided a Webinar series for seasoned alumni to help them launch a new chapter built around generativity. And organizations are emerging to centralize opportunities and counsel for midlife transition in certain geographies—Coming of Age in Philadelphia and now several other cities; Life by Design NW in Portland, Oregon; SHiFT in Minneapolis; and Tempe Connections in Arizona, to name just a few.

Another development in recent years is the appearance of a life-coaching profession focused on helping people entering the new stage. In the past, those seeking planning help at this point might have talked primarily to retirement planners and financial advisers. But today, career and life coaches are focused on questions of meaning, purpose, vocation, and the process of making a big change—and more and more financial planners are themselves trying to adapt their skills and get into the act.

In 2005 a group of forward-thinking coaches formed the Life Planning Network, a national alliance of coaches providing "professional development, support, and opportunities to shape the burgeoning field of third-age life planning." Its goal: "to bring life planning into the mainstream and to advance the cause of self- and social renewal in the third age."

There's no doubt that many involved in these developments— in my experience, most—are motivated to help individuals moving into the new stage find greater fulfillment and expand their contribution. At the same time, the growth of activity marks another important development: The transition of tens of millions constitutes a sizable market.

SCHOOL FOR THE SECOND HALF OF LIFE

Mark Noonan didn't make his transition to a whole new chapter in life through a support group or personal adviser. Much of the process he went through took place at home, late at night, in front of his computer. And the vehicle was a community college program aimed at helping boomers find a new life direction after fifty.

The trigger for Noonan's change was, unfortunately, tragic news from home. He was on a three-week business trip to China when he heard that his wife had fallen at home and died. The engineer, in his fifties at the time, got on the next plane home to Portland, Oregon. Flying back, he was in a stunned state, trying to assimilate the news, beginning to mourn, thinking about what this all meant. "All the grieving and mourning sent me spinning, about what was the purpose of life," Noonan recalls. "I did a lot of reflecting." He had become increasingly uncomfortable with his work, much of it involving downsizing plants, a real-life version of the *Up in the Air* script. "And I felt my work was more about tearing down communities and breaking up families. Is that what I really wanted to do?"

It was 2004, and Noonan spent two more years with the company. "Then, at a certain point, I just realized I didn't have the heart for it anymore," he says. Noonan approached management and asked for a severance package. Because his company was outsourcing jobs to China and elsewhere, federal money was available to help with his transition. He now recalls that there was a certain amount of expedience to his decision, as well; he could see that the kind of downsizing that he had been carrying out would soon be carried out—on him.

Noonan approached this change like an engineer, doing market research, talking to people, playing out different options in his head. When he was done, he made a decision that involved a fair bit of logic. He studied future trends, including demographics, and decided to pursue a second act in gerontology. "As I started exploring the gerontology world, I started having an excitement I haven't had since I told my friends I was going off to electronics school in 1973." He says that he made his move not necessarily from "wanting to help older people. It was more from pure potential . . . what I thought will be some real job opportunities."

Although he already had a bachelor's degree, Noonan enrolled in Portland Community College's initiative aimed at helping Encore Stage adults transition into human service careers. The community college route was "quick, fast, and efficient." It was also cheap—no small virtue in today's economy. Noonan earned an associate degree in gerontology in eighteen months—reversing another old pattern, that you get such a degree en route to a BA or BS.

Although it all seems logical now, Noonan admits that it didn't feel comfortable much of the time. "It was very intimidating to think about going back to school," he reflects, "the idea of being on campus and . . . being the only white-haired person in the class." The project offered him the option of doing his work online, which suited his schedule—Noonan felt he was most productive from 10 p.m. to 1 a.m. anyway. "You get the same lecture, reading, discussion, testing, as someone taking the class in person," he says. "I had great discussions online with people I never met. It's really the future."

Counterbalancing Noonan's online learning, experiencing, and helping make the transition more than theoretical, were a trio of internships: one with the local Meals on Wheels program, another with AARP in Oregon, and a third with a human services agency called Elders in Action. That third internship turned into a job, one that seems to bring together his past high-tech life and his new gerontology career, in true looking backward–giving forward fashion. Noonan now works as the inaugural social media manager for Elders in Action, where he is building up the presence of the organization—an advocacy and social service group for the elderly—on Facebook and Twitter.

Community colleges are increasingly focusing on the encore market not just for enrichment (think: watercolors) but for life transition and job training, particularly attuned to places where the jobs are projected to be—health care, education, the emerging green economy, and, yes, aging. And there will be more, given the leadership role the American Association of Community Colleges appears to be taking and the demographics themselves. (When my organization, Civic Ventures, offered modest funds to community colleges around the country to develop pathways along these lines, hundreds of community colleges lined up, ten applying for every available grant.)

Continuing education programs, typically at four-year universities, are also getting in on the action. One of the pioneers is the University of Minnesota, which offers an Encore Transitions program to help people prepare for a new stage of life by "focusing on personal, professional, and social satisfaction, as well as financial preparation." It's taught by university faculty, life coaches, financial planners, and other experts.

Some graduate programs being developed focus explicitly on new stagers. For example, Washington University in St. Louis has proposed the creation of an Executive MSW program aimed at boomers making a career and life shift, while Cranfield School of Management in the UK is exploring the establishment of a Third Age MBA.

Not all the models are new, either. For many years, without much fanfare, a number of colleges have operated programs aimed at older "nontraditional" students—many in the encore years. For example, at Wellesley, the Davis Degree Program gives women well past traditional undergraduate age the chance to come back to school, be integrated in the college community, yet also maintain a peer group of older students. They get help with orientation and academic support, and even have their own CE (for Continuing Education) House with a furnished living room and kitchen. Most have already had some college but are returning to complete their degrees. Since the early 1970s, more than eight hundred alumnae have graduated through the program. Similar models exist at Mount Holyoke, the State University of New York, and elsewhere.

One of my favorite variations is the Sacred Heart School of Theology in Hales Corners, Wisconsin, which educates Catholic priests. Faced with a declining applicant pool from the traditional group of young men coming out of high school, and confronting formidable debt payments on recently completed campus buildings, the seminary drew on necessity as the impetus for invention. They began recruiting widowers, men who had already been married, usually had families, and lost their wives. They were moving into a new phase of life and interested in devoting their lives to spiritual priorities. Today, a significant segment of the Sacred Heart student body consists of these second-act seminarians—and the school offers a new model for religious education.

One of the most ambitious and impressive innovations in the higher-education spectrum targeting new stagers is Harvard's Advanced Leadership Initiative (ALI), aimed at helping high achievers develop new ideas to solve the world's biggest problems. The program is the brainchild of three leading lights at the university's business school, former *Harvard Business Review* editor and management scholar Rosabeth Moss Kanter, who heads the initiative; Dean Nitin Nohria; and Professor Rakesh Khurana.

The ten-month program (part-time in residence) combines participation in Harvard classes, exposure to "think tanks" led by affiliated faculty on topics of major global concern, and the chance to develop an entrepreneurial project aimed at solving a pressing social problem.

The talent of some of the early enrollees (fourteen were in the inaugural class) reflects well on the Harvard name. Retired Marine Corps major general Charles Bolden, sixty-two, was tapped in the middle of his ALI term to head up NASA. Jamie Kaplan, a former corporate lawyer, completed the program and is now executive director of the Cromwell Center for Disabilities Awareness in Portland, Maine. Another student, ex-Trader Joe's president Doug Rauch, is now working on strategies to end food waste and to change people's eating habits to promote wellness.

From online classes to community college certificate programs, from continuing education courses to graduate schools for the best and the brightest, it is possible to see the contours of a new kind of higher education in America—the inklings of what could become school for the second half of life.

FEET IN THE DOOR

John Armstrong's life has been characterized by successive waves of service, going back to his Boy Scout years. After graduating from West Point, like his father and his grandfather and great-grandfather before him, Armstrong—a towering figure, with the bearing of a Canadian Mountie—spent six years in the U.S. Army. When he finished his tour (he was stationed in Germany when the Berlin Wall came down), Armstrong got an MBA at the University of Washington in Seattle, worked for a decade as a financial analyst in the corporate world, and then put in five years at Hewlett-Packard.

As Armstrong approached forty, he and his wife joined the Peace Corps, where he served as a marketing adviser in Slovakia, helping to build up civil society there. Despite his lack of marketing experience, he was billed as "the marketing expert from America" to the mayor of Veloen, the town where he was placed by the Peace Corps. It meant giving up his job at HP, but as it turns out, he was able to get rehired when he returned. Actually, he got a better job, at a higher salary—in marketing!

A few years later, Armstrong was laid off as part of a 10 percent across-the-board cutback of staff, the first of a series of layoffs at the computer company. He got a severance package that essentially bought him a year off, which he vowed to use to make the move to the nonprofit sector. "I just figured it was a natural extension of what I had been doing," he recalls. "I had been in the military. I had served in the Peace Corps. When I came back from the Peace Corps, I volunteered at Eastside College Preparatory School in East Palo Alto for years."

Then his plans got deferred again when a friend from HP called him up and asked if he wanted to work on a two-week project. It turned into another full-time job at the company. Four years later he was ready to try a shift again. Acting on that decision was made much easier by the health coverage he had through his wife's job as a librarian at Stanford.

As a route into the nonprofit world, Armstrong started taking courses and volunteering at organizations, but it was "all unstructured—there was no focus, no direction." Then a former colleague at HP called to recruit Armstrong, not for another round back at the company but for a new pilot project, the Silicon Valley Encore Fellows program.

The project was designed to test the theory that paid internships could actually work for people in the encore phase of life. (Full disclosure: The Encore Fellows program was created by Civic Ventures.) Our hope was that these new pathways could help individuals like Armstrong figure out how to transition to an encore career in the nonprofit sector—to translate pertinent skills like marketing, human resources, and information technology that are as needed in the world of nonprofits as in the for-profit arena. "You think, well, I worked at Hewlett-Packard, I've got a lot of skills, any nonprofit would love me," Armstrong reflects. But that didn't turn out to be the case. Nonprofit employers were skeptical about whether those skills would translate and whether he could navigate a new culture.

In an attempt to cross this divide through the fellowship (essentially an internship for grown-ups), Armstrong got to interview with a set of nonprofits in the two areas he most cared about, education and the environment. He selected a hybrid— Environmental Volunteers, an environmental education program focused on public elementary schools. "I'm the marketing expert from America, again," Armstrong laughs. His assignment: to raise the profile of the organization.

Armstrong's fellowship combined both on-the-job training and peer support. Each month, the ten fellows in Silicon Valley got together to share experiences and listen to talks by experts on topics such as the nonprofit sector and midlife transition. Often, their managers, the nonprofit executive directors, came, too. A goal of the project is to change the hiring practices of those organizations, by exposing them to a new talent source that adds value. There's a bit of a Trojan-horse quality to the model.

And there are signs that this arrangement leads to payoffs: At the end of the first year of the program, 90 percent of the fellows received—and accepted—job offers from nonprofits. Armstrong is now the collaborations project manager at Environmental Volunteers, heading up "Science by Nature."

Will this innovation be scalable? Can it work in other communities with people of various backgrounds and organizations that are more resistant? It's too early to know. One thing is encouraging: The Encore Fellows approach squares with extensive research about what leads to successful real-world work transitions across the life course. "We like to think that the key to a successful career change is knowing what we want to do next, then using that knowledge to guide our actions," writes Herminia Ibarra, author of *Working Identity* and a professor at the European business school INSEAD. "But studying people in the throes of the career change process . . . led me to a startling conclusion," Ibarra continues. "Change actually happens the other way around. Doing comes first, knowing second."

For all these reasons it is heartening to see more internships popping up later in the life course. According to a CareerBuilder survey from the summer of 2010, nearly a quarter of employers report getting internship applications by individuals over fifty or other "experienced workers," reshaping the role of internships in the process.

Another emerging internship-esque path is national service. Programs like the Peace Corps, VISTA, and AmeriCorps—which already have a track record of serving as transition vehicles for young people—are enrolling more and more individuals in their encore years. Experience Corps, targeted to individuals over fifty-five and part of the AmeriCorps network of opportunities, is one example. A growing number of Experience Corps members are using their time in the program not just to provide intensive service to low-income children and schools but also to launch a new chapter in the education field.

Michael Burke spent nearly two decades as a cook, working on his feet in demanding physical labor until he reached the point where his body began giving out. "When you cook, you tend to work prime time. You're working Sundays, you're working weekends, you're working nights, you're standing up all day, and I was realizing that this was just too much for me. My arthritis began to get bad, and I just couldn't take it, you know," he said.

After talking to his pastor and doing volunteer work, he joined Experience Corps in Baltimore. Working fifteen hours a week mentoring and tutoring for a small stipend turned out to be the start of Burke's encore career. At first, Burke said he "felt intimidated because I didn't know if the children were going to like me. I kept thinking I would get upset one day and start yelling at them. I really did. I didn't know what was going to happen. But those kids actually changed me. . . . I realized that I was a good person with children, that I had a lot inside of me that children needed."

Burke simultaneously took classes at the Community College of Baltimore County, before getting hired as Experience Corps' training coordinator. Service had served as a gateway to a new job and a new identity, really to a new phase of life.

A SCHOOL FOR LIFE?

Peter Laslett looked to America as the wellspring for new ideas that would create the institutions needed to help usher people into the Third Age. There's no question that the United States is good at social innovation, although it certainly owns no monopoly on creativity in this area. It's a good thing, too, given that the new stage is a global phenomenon. In fact, one of the most promising prototypes for a next-generation transition vehicle is under way in London.

In early 2010, while researching the rise of the Third Age concept in the United Kingdom, I was introduced to a unique innovation that's a combination of continuing education, a transition support group, and something of a secular religion. The School of Life is located in a storefront in Bloomsbury, a block from Russell Square, in the shadows of University College, London. It was created by British writer Alain de Botton, author of *The Pleasures and Sorrows of Work*, and travel writer Geoff Dyer. The attractive first floor of the shop is a bookstore, but not an ordinary one. The carefully culled collection—"all the essential books on all the great topics crucial to leading a good life"—is organized by theme, with topics like "how to enjoy your own company," "how to make a difference," or "how to survive insomnia." There are no more than six titles on each topic.

Classes at the School of Life follow a similarly boiled-down, essential quality, blending the high life of the mind with the practicalities of actually living a good life. It's organized around the central themes of love, work, death, and other big questions.

Among the classes: How to Balance Work with Life, How to Be a Good Friend, How to Have Better Conversations, How to Make Love Last, How to Spend Time Alone, How to Fill the God-Shaped Hole, How to Face Death, and, my favorite (and probably most desperately needed), How to Be Cool. Along with these classes, the School of Life offers special weekend workshops; lectures on fundamental issues like loss, innovation, and mindfulness; as well as psychotherapy ("Our aim is to take you on a fascinating and valuable tour of your own psyche").

In addition to talk therapy of the psychological sort, the School of Life offers something unique: bibliotherapy—designed to help you figure out what to read in an era when two new books are published every minute, "and you would need 163 lifetimes to get through all the titles offered on Amazon." An appointment with a School of Life "bibliotherapist" is encouraged for those seeking to improve their reading life, resulting in a "reading prescription," whether "you're looking for a set of travel novels to inspire your next adventure, or you'd like to fathom an aspect of a current relationship through a short collection of essays."

An additional arrow in the School of Life's quiver is a Sunday sermon series delivered by prominent cultural figures in the UK and dedicated (for the most part) to spiritual ideas and other fundamental questions. Attendees are told to "expect hellfire preaching, an alternative parish newsletter, hymns, sticky buns, conversations with fellow 'parishioners' and the possible appearance of the Devil himself."

That same trip I decided to take a weekend School of Life class on finding more meaningful work. I was surprised to be joined in the group of ten by two doctors, one from the UK and another from Germany, another German working for a cultural society, a Dutch management consultant, a Spanish business reporter, an American who worked for big corporations in the UK, and an advertising manager at a global agency. The group, along with the instructor, was overwhelmingly weighted toward the encore phase.

On Sunday morning I played hooky from the weekend class to attend a School of Life sermon on the subject of perspective by Charles Leadbeater, the former *Independent* journalist, the editor who commissioned *Bridget Jones's Diary*, and one of the UK's leading authorities on innovation. At 11:30 a.m., I arrived in Conway Hall—an ethical society in Bloomsbury's Red Lion Square established in the nineteenth century by an American abolitionist living in Britain—to discover hundreds of people already filtering into pews, each paying the equivalent of twenty dollars. The crowd spanned the age spectrum. Every seat on the ground floor and every space in the balcony was taken. At precisely 11:45, an attractive twentysomething folksinger walked up to the stage, we all stood, and she sang a version of Crosby, Stills, Nash & Young's "Teach Your Children."

Leadbeater then gave a rousing talk, arguing we would all benefit by thinking about our lives from back to front, reflecting on what a good old age and death would look like, then using that perspective to guide how we live forward to that goal. The advertisement for the talk had stated: "Charles isn't suffering a mid-life crisis"; rather, he'd come to the conclusion that while "the values of youth are about possession, consumption, expression and individuality, the values that underpin dignity in age and death are about relationships, connectedness, sharing and participation—far more powerful drivers for social change."

Forty-five minutes later, Leadbeater exited the stage to a standing ovation. We all remained on our feet as the same young folksinger returned and sang, appropriately, the Beatles' "When I'm Sixty-Four." Then everyone left for the advertised sticky buns and conversation.

I left thinking. Maybe that's the best way to state the value of the School of Life experience. I left thinking about my own life, about social innovations we could be launching, and about how useful it would be if many of these innovations designed to help us make the shift to a new stage of life could be brought together in a holistic way. We're making progress in this direction, we're moving from a do-it-yourself shift to something less DIY. Still, the opportunities are mostly piecemeal.

With a generation of fifty- and sixtysomethings poised to make this very difficult transition, the options shouldn't be so fragmented or arduous. The variations described above—in planning, education, internships, and service opportunities—provide a glimpse of how it could be easier. They suggest a time when people like Paula Lopez Crespin and John Kerr won't have to sneak into pathways designed for their children. They show how we could begin crafting a front door, in place of the circuitous routes so commonplace today, a main entrance big enough to accommodate the vast opportunity headed our way.

SEVEN

Ten Steps Toward a New Stage

· ·

Carl Jung argued that "a human being would certainly not grow to be 70 or 80 years old if this longevity has no meaning for the species." Others too believe that the bonus decades beyond fifty or sixty, and the opportunity presented by them, are no accident. In her groundbreaking "Grandmother Hypothesis," Kristen Hawkes of the University of Utah puts forth the theory that grandmothers in particular played a critical role in helping humans survive and flourish as a species. Other researchers suggest that adults in the postreproductive years who were skilled in social relationships and cohesiveness probably did much to increase survival prospects for their descendants and for humans more broadly.

In other words, the perfect storm of conditions lining up to support the development of a new stage between the middle years and old age has, in certain respects at least, been brewing for a long time, a very long time. This extended trajectory brings with it a reminder that we need to be thinking longer term, perhaps asking the question that Jonas Salk raised, namely, "Are we being good ancestors?"

Still, evolutionary forces alone won't inexorably produce the encore stage or the desired new map of life. That's going to be up to us. As I've said, life stages are social construction projects. There's nothing natural or determined about them. We create new stages deliberately in order to solve problems, to bring more sense to the world, to reflect our deepest values. That's the way it's always been.

So how do we turn the period that's been opening beyond midlife from a season all too often characterized by identity void, economic disengagement, and societal confusion into something that has a shot of being the new crown of life? And how do we ensure that the best thing that ever happened to us as individuals, the prospect of extended and healthier lives, is a boon to the broader community, now and into the future?

It's a daunting assignment, creating a life stage and rewriting the course of life. There's a certain amount of hubris involved in even contemplating the task. Fortunately, we don't have to start from scratch. We have past experience as a guide, through obvious examples like the invention of retirement and the creation of childhood and adolescence. And the models don't stop with the existing stages of life. Even concepts like parenthood offer useful lessons.

Historian Jill Lepore suggests that parenthood, seemingly always and ever-present—how can you have human beings without parenthood?—was itself a social invention and a relatively recent one at that. For much of our history, children were born when parents were very young, and they kept coming until there were ten or twelve of them, with some invariably at home when (a typically early) death came calling for the parents. In Lepore's telling, in eighteenth- and nineteenth-century America, "to be an adult was to be a parent."

By the turn of the twentieth century, that was all changing, driven in part by much smaller households and increasingly longer lives. As a result, the segment of the adult population who *weren't* parents grew sharply. There became a phase of life when the kids were grown and the parents were still around—and that meant parenthood became a distinct category. What's more, as Americans became geographically mobile, families could no longer count on relatives to pass on knowledge about how to be a good parent—how to change a baby's diapers or discipline a child.

Into the breach came a wave of parenting experts, among them G. Stanley Hall, who helped establish the field of child study in the United States. Other innovations followed. Pediatrics was in the midst of becoming a specialty. The Children's Bureau of the federal government was established in 1912, and *Parents* magazine was formed in the 1920s (under an earlier name). Advice literature filled the bookstore shelves, along with a raft of other products, manuals, organizations, and agencies. Soon it appeared that parenthood was an indelible feature of the social landscape, one that was assumed to have always been so.

In contemplating the development of life stages and related categories, like parenthood, it's clear that social inventions require

new ways of thinking, new social arrangements, and new movements for change. Throw in growing discomfort on the part of
individuals in the prospective category, and the perception that
the group in question poses a big problem if things don't change,
and pretty soon something comes to exist in a space that was
once awkward and empty.

Today's prescription for development of the Encore Stage
seems no different. Just as important, as we contemplate what
the future landscape might and should look like, it's heartening
to know that change is already under way through the impact of
role models like Meredith McKenzie and Paula Lopez Crespin,
Mark Noonan and Michael Burke, along with their organizational equivalents, groups including the Transition Network, the
Encore Fellowships Network, the Advanced Leadership Initiative,
and the School of Life. That's progress and a source of inspiration. They are not only signals from the future—but for it!

Now it's time to shift into a higher gear. We must move beyond the vanguard of pioneering individuals and leading-edge
innovations, mostly small in number and in scale, to get more
people and more institutions involved in realizing the promise
of the new period. We're talking about tens of millions of women
and men facing a potential chasm, in need of something better.

While the contours of what's needed are evident, it's hard to
know exactly what the breakthrough approaches will end up
being. The remapping of life is rarely an orderly, or linear, process.
Who would have guessed a golf course and some Levittown-style
houses in the middle of a forsaken Arizona cotton field would
produce the institution that defined the golden years? For that

matter, who would have imagined that a turn-of-the-twentieth-century thousand-page academic opus, with the distinctly unpoetic title of *Adolescence*, would have served as a prescription and label for the years between childhood and adulthood?

The main lesson is that if we are to produce the "optimal design for a new stage of life," in Laura Carstensen's words, one that builds on its assets and accounts for potential perils, we'll need to dramatically raise the pace of innovation.

GETTING STARTED

Here are ten approaches that hold promise, individually and in various combinations and permutations, to carry us forward toward the next map of life.

1. **Think Differently.** We must shake loose from the tyranny of dead ideas, from the old patterns that compromise our ability to think imaginatively about the period between midlife and old age. That means resisting the temptation to see this time as a version of something else—whether that's endless midlife, reinvented retirement, or a flavor of old age, coming in young-old, not-so-young-old, oldest-old, and other variations.

At the individual level it's almost as if the GPS program guiding our journey across the life course has to be reset and reprogrammed. Now as we try to move into new chapters, the messages inside and out tell us to return to established paths, to recalculate our route, to circle back to the familiar. But all too often that voice is leading us toward a dead end. It will take courage and creativity to navigate a new path.

As a society, going a different way means disruption. The old way of thinking (and acting) has its defenders—and its constituency. Beyond inertia, there are vested interests in things not changing one bit. The stakes are significant. Creating the new stage would by definition peel prestige and resources away from many industries and groups, most notably those in the retirement and aging industries. What if they were suddenly left with a quarter of the population they currently claim? A small fraction of the market?

None of this is to suggest that investment in, care of, research on, housing for, and advocacy on behalf of the elderly shouldn't be a top priority. (As Peter Laslett reminds us, that's as much enlightened self-interest as good ethics: We'll all be there soon enough!) However, reclassifying those new stagers who never should have been lumped in this category in the first place will mean great upheaval—and pitched battles may well ensue. Yet that is exactly what needs to happen.

2. **Create the Category.** Just as we must break free of old ideas tethered to a now-defunct chart of life, we need to embrace new ones suited to contemporary circumstances. That means launching the new stage with a new dream for this period, a new definition of success, and new language to establish the integrity and weight of this time of life.

We could start, as many such ideas do, with a commission of experts. I know, I know, not another commission. A body of this sort could hardly be counted on to single-handedly put the new map on the map. However, it could do much to establish the En-core Stage among thought and opinion leaders. More substantively, there is value in looking at how best to design this period, much as the MacArthur Foundation has done through a series of commissions on other periods of life including childhood, emerging adulthood, midlife, and the later years. (It is worth noting that the MacArthur midlife commission defined its domain as thirty-five to seventy, and its commission on the aging society includes many of the same years in its mandate. The new stage sits precariously at the intersection of the two panels.) In my view, the new stage between midlife and old age deserves its own inquiry—as it was given through the prescient Carnegie Inquiry on the Third Age in Britain decades ago.

There are other ways we can start to create the category apart from an august convening. The academic study of the encore phase, now mostly gathered under gerontology, could become its own group, with its own academic association equivalent to the Gerontological Society of America. And all those working in the new stage vineyard, from life coaches to health navigators, might have their own group to advance practices and professional standards.

Our culture needs to do more to send signals about this emerging period, marking its existence and establishing a vision for it. Certainly, *More* magazine (despite its reinvention bent) and the TNT television show *Men of a Certain Age* (for all its angst) constitute two commercially successful variations on how this might be done. Another sign is the development of AARP's awards for "movies for grown-ups" and its marketing campaign featuring individuals over fifty explaining what they'd like to do "when they grow up."

And, of course, the rise in intellectual interest and writing about the new stage in thoughtful books about the subject, like Sara Lawrence-Lightfoot's eloquent *The Third Chapter* and Mary Catherine Bateson's landmark *Composing a Further Life*, is an important development. Now if we could only develop a distinct section of the bookstore for them rather than sandwiching the subject between guides for retiring in the Yucatán and puzzles aimed at warding off dementia.

3. **A Gap Year for Grown-Ups.** If we're already in the habit of adapting approaches—like school and internships—designed for young people, why stop there? The gap year has become an important rite of passage for youth on their journey to adulthood and an opportunity to gain the new perspective necessary for making the most of what's next. It's also a time for renewal, an opportunity for stressed-out and worn-out young people to catch their breath before tackling college, graduate school, or the rigors of the working world.

For all these reasons, a gap period in the space between the middle years and the emerging stage is an attractive proposition. A gap year for grown-ups would offer the chance for reflection, renewal, and redirection. It would provide an opportunity to disrupt familiar patterns (and inertia), to grow personally, to be exposed to new experiences, and to try on potential future roles. The gap year could provide the kind of pause, or foundation, people need to start a new stage of life. As mentioned earlier, at Civic Ventures we've employed the semicolon and the construct "then; now" to symbolize the transition between middle age (then) and the encore phase (now). The semicolon is an alternative both to the period, designating an ending, and the comma, a brief pause along the way. The semicolon suggests continuity, a genuine break, and more to come. For a life course in desperate need of punctuation, the grown-up gap year is the perfect way to rectify the run-on sentence.

Many people are already taking time off, in one form or another. Some even call it retirement. A 2010 study from the RAND Corporation shows that a sizable portion of the U.S. population first retires and then "unretires," an act researchers find is primarily by design and not the result of unexpected circumstances. In other words, many may be using the cover of retirement, followed by unretirement, as a kind of de facto gap period. And these interludes are hardly exclusive to the United States. In Britain, for example, there are an estimated 200,000 "grey gappers" taking a career break, according to one report.

Daniel Pink suggests we "take a Sagmeister," not only in the postmidlife period but regularly throughout the life course. He didn't just make that word up. It's based on the practice of designer Stefan Sagmeister, who, in Pink's telling, decided that the old regimen of twenty-five years of education, then forty of working, then twenty-five of leisured retirement didn't cut it. His innovation: Take a chunk of those retirement years and allocate them throughout the life course, building in time for new learning, growth, disruption, and renewal every seven years or so. That's what academics do, for example, and they don't even have to call it a Sagmeister.

Some individuals in their fifties and sixties are in a position to take their gap year—whether they've "retired" from a career, have been downsized, or are taking a breather before "unretiring." Others might want to do a stealth gap year, along the lines of an executive education program. Imagine a version that one could take without quitting one's job or telling your boss, using holidays, weekends, and vacation time. It might include trying a "vocation vacation" (pioneered by entrepreneur Brian Kurth) that provides weeklong internships in a potentially appealing second career, like working on animal welfare or in a bakery. That week could be combined over a period of months with an academic course, as well as some volunteer experiences and adventure travel to create a period of renewal and reevaluation, especially if life and career coaching are added to the mix.

Get real, you're thinking. Most Americans in the postmidlife phase won't be able to afford a gap year. I agree, which is why I believe we as a society need to do more to help people take the time they need to regroup for a productive new stage. I discuss this further in steps 7, 8, and 9 below.

4. **Highest Education.** A key part of preparing for the encore phase, gap year or not, is supporting continued development—including human-capital development and retraining to enhance and enable continued contribution. We have a long history of educational innovation, including the development of lifelong learning programs aimed at the over-sixty population. Beginning in

the 1970s, Elderhostel (now known as Road Scholar) created an entirely new education model for "older people" aimed at self-development. Since the early days, that organization has helped spawn a multibillion-dollar industry and changed the culture to make learning in the second half of life a common aspiration. The University of the Third Age, U3A in the UK, has achieved similar progress. Likewise, the adult education industry has proliferated in recent decades, including efforts like the University of Phoenix, Capella, Kaplan, and Walden.

Now is the time to develop a new kind of education suited to the new stage of life, blending vocational preparation, personal transformation, and intellectual stimulation. Initiatives like the Advanced Leadership Initiative at Harvard, the sustainability MBAs at Bainbridge Graduate Institute and the Presidio Graduate School, and the Fielding Graduate University, among others, are pioneering this model. Increasingly, alumni associations and continuing education and community college programs are also leading the way. A whole new higher-education sector is beginning to emerge. We must do everything possible to complete this process.

The old model simply doesn't make sense for a one hundred–year life span. Why invest all our higher-education time and the vast majority of our higher-education dollars in the eighteen- to twenty-five period when people are going to live for sixty or seventy-five more years and work for a good fifty or sixty of those years? Why not go to school for a period of years after high school, stay engaged in education all along the way, and then go again more intensively thirty years down the road? It's hard to know at twenty what you'll want to do at fifty or sixty or what the appealing options will even be.

Just as the timing of education will need to change—and perhaps the credentials with it—so too will the nature of learning. Sixty-year-olds learn in different ways than sixteen-year-olds, and experiential learning is much better suited to the latter years. New technologies are also producing new possibilities, especially through the unbundling of educational services and offerings. In fact, the extraordinary education opportunity emerging around the encore years may serve as a catalyst for changing the entire way the nation approaches higher education, making it far more adaptable to people at all stages of life.

As Harvard's Rosabeth Moss Kanter has argued, "third-stage education" would "give higher education a transformational concept and a catalytic innovation" for its own next chapter— innovations capable of ushering in "an era of integrative knowledge to solve twenty-first century problems while facilitating the social invention of a new life stage."

5. **National Service, Redux.** National service programs—most notably the Peace Corps, the most memorable innovation introduced in President Kennedy's "Ask not" speech—were designed for young people. Now the very people the Peace Corps was created to engage are themselves at the new stage, and many are looking for another round of service with the same motivations that young people bring to the job: to give back, to have an adventure, to acquire experience, and to gain the credentials and credibility to launch a new chapter of life and work.

Some, like Gary Maxworthy, who wanted to join the Peace Corps when he was younger, have seized a second chance through programs like AmeriCorps. Leslie Hawke is another example. As she approached fifty, she joined the Peace Corps and was assigned to Romania. After a year, and the persistence of a boy named Alex who begged at Hawke's window, Hawke began to raise money to help "get the poorest kids into school so they might have a chance to become productive, responsible members of society." Like Maxworthy, Hawke's initial step of service led to becoming a social entrepreneur, to starting an organization to make enduring change. In the ten years since The Alex Fund, Hawke's foundation, was established, it has helped mothers gain skills and find jobs so their children will be freed up to go to school, supported efforts to equalize educational opportunities in some of the very poorest sections of Romania, and sponsored a public-awareness campaign aimed at parents.

Whereas some like Maxworthy and Hawke followed the entrepreneurial path, for others like Michael Burke or John Armstrong, national service is a route to a second career. Recognizing the potential of these examples, the 2010 Edward M. Kennedy Serve America Act calls for expanding the number of new-stage AmeriCorps members—in effect, to integrate the program by age. The law sets a target of 10 percent for the proportion of AmeriCorps members over fifty-five, which could soon mean 25,000 individuals if AmeriCorps—the nation's signature service program—reaches full strength. But why stop at 10 percent? Why not a quarter or a third or even half? If more people will soon be over sixty than under twenty, shouldn't these Americans have just as many opportunities to serve—and to transition to new careers—as their younger counterparts?

The Serve America Act also includes a provision establishing ten encore fellowships in each state, a high-profile way to spread the idea and demonstrate the potential of encore fellowships far and wide. But these five hundred new fellowships, designed specifically to help those in the encore transition to work we need done in fields from education to health care and the environment, have yet to be funded. It's time to honor the intent of the legislation, time to make the best use of the experience that's so clearly out there.

6. **Elevate Encore Careers.** Work will be a core and defining feature of the new stage. But the extension of working lives, along with longer lives in general, has left us somewhat confused about what work should look like in this period.

Encore careers, a version of "what's next" at the confluence of money, meaning, and social impact, represent in my view the highest form of contribution during this period. Most people need or want to work longer, but many don't want to do the same thing they've been doing—or don't have the option of staying the midlife course. They need to earn an income, but they want new work they feel good about, work that plows their experience into something lasting, something that improves the quality of life in their communities.

Encore careers have already developed a powerful following. One study shows that nearly 10 million boomers have moved into second careers in areas like education, the environment, health, and social services, while fully half of those who haven't already made the move say that it's a top priority for their next phase. What's more, labor economist Barry Bluestone of Northeastern University shows that if the economy recovers at even a modest rate, there will be profound labor shortages by the year 2018 in the exact same career areas that these individuals aspire to pursue. (That should help alleviate some concerns about this population displacing young people in the labor market—a perspective that wrongly assumes these groups are competing for the same jobs anyway.)

Encore careers are to the new stage what leisure was to retirement: the goal, a way of turning necessity into a virtue. We need to construct a deal around these kinds of longer working lives that's as powerful as the one we crafted to realize shorter working lives a half century ago. Doing so will turn the push (you have to work longer) into a pull (there's important work you want to do). It will turn the old dream of the freedom *from* work into a new dream, the freedom *to* work.

But, for millions of Americans, making the shift from a midlife career to an encore one, like so much else about shifting into the new stage, is too daunting, too hard to finance, and too difficult to find—especially in the current economic climate. We need to make it easier for people to pursue opportunities in the second half of their working lives that are fulfilling and have an impact, especially options that enable individuals to move up the economic and social ladder.

7. **Revamp HR Policies.** Employers can get in on the innovation act more fully by creating new policies and practices that help employees transition to a new stage of work and life. Some ideas in this arena are simple and obvious and help employees find and stay in jobs longer. These include flextime to care for aging parents or grandchildren, part-time or part-year jobs, training to help employees update their skills, and, of course, an end to subtle and not-so-subtle age discrimination in hiring. Other policies and practices are more complex and involve helping employees make the transition to encore careers and other new stage pursuits.

In their article in *Harvard Business Review*, "The Existential Necessity of Midlife Change," Carlo Strenger and Arie Ruttenberg argue that "organizations need to take radical steps" to enable employees to "understand that given current life expectancy, everybody in the company will leave at some point and begin a second life. The only question is at what age." To help ease transitions, they write, "companies must help executives prepare for a second life as a matter of policy." They suggest providing coaches or consultants to help employees plan their second careers, establishing a continuing education fund for personal development, collaborating with colleges to develop new transition programs for executives, and the like. "Of course," Strenger and Ruttenberg write, "such investments cost money, but the return is invaluable for as long as the executive stays at the company." Even if focused on postemployment transition, such investments may give a company a competitive edge in hiring. Who wouldn't want to work for an organization that was willing to invest in his or her next chapter?

IBM is one company breaking new ground in this area, having initially created the Transition to Teaching program to help its employees shift to jobs as math and science teachers. The company has since launched vehicles to help employees transition to jobs in government and the nonprofit sector. Meanwhile, one-time math teacher and former Paramount Pictures CEO Sherry Lansing has created the EnCorps Teaching program in California, enabling companies to help former engineering and high-tech workers move into new chapters teaching math and science in public schools.

As the Encore Fellowship initiative underscores, Hewlett-Packard has likewise been a pioneer in corporate innovation for the new stage, backing the first fellowship pilot in Silicon Valley. Now Intel, Agilent, and other major corporations have joined in the effort, helping former employees take important steps toward a new stage—simultaneously extending their impact in the community.

These efforts exemplify a compelling alternative to traditional corporate retirement planning for employees—and should become standard operating procedure.

8. Individual Purpose Accounts (and More). Over the past few years I've heard stories of boomers who were tapping into their children's 529 accounts to go back to school themselves. It's totally legal and understandable, given the absence of any established savings vehicles to help fund postmidlife transitions. But why not fill the void? Why should we save all our money for an extended period of not working, for retirement, when what many really need are savings to cover the costs of more transition periods in life, most especially the one leading into the encore years? We should be saving for this shift, inevitable for many people and expensive too, given the cost of going back to school or living without a full salary during a gap year or fellowship.

Financial advisers are beginning to recommend that individuals set up special savings accounts to help them manage their encore transitions. Segregating funds from individual retirement accounts can preserve traditional retirement security while accumulating resources to invest in a new stage of life and work. Since society has so much at stake in such a large segment of the population finding its footing postmidlife, we should be creating tax-advantaged vehicles like the IRA to help fund this transition. What about an IPA—an Individual Purpose Account aimed at the transition or transitions in one's fifties and sixties? With tax credits and other mechanisms, Congress could support individual purpose accounts as distinct packages designed to make switching to encore careers easier, just as 401(k)s make saving for retirement easier. Financial institutions are well placed to offer individual purpose accounts (IPAs) that integrate, streamline, and automate the processes for taking advantage of tax treatments, employer matches, investment options, loan programs, and other incentives. Proposals exist for many of the needed pieces for such accounts.

IPAs could be both a policy opportunity and also a potential bonanza for the private sector, which is offering retirement products but little in the way of savings vehicles for alternative approaches to the last two, three, or four decades of life. As a result, people are turning to more back-door approaches, like the 529 bandits described above. A side benefit: If the financial-services companies become more involved in developing these products, their marketing muscle is likely to go far in putting the new stage on the map.

Another idea, embodied in the Lifelong Learning Accounts Act of 2007 introduced by Senators Maria Cantwell and Olympia Snowe, would help workers save for future education to jump-start encore careers. Modeled on a program already in place at IBM, the bill would establish tax-exempt lifelong learning accounts (LiLAs) to pay for certain educational expenses, including tuition, fees, books, supplies, and information technology devices; provide individuals with a tax credit for cash contributions to their LiLAs; and allow employers a tax credit for contributions they make to the LiLAs of their employees.

Finally, student financial-aid policies also have to be revamped to support encore transitions. Existing financial aid disadvantages part-time students, including individuals who have family obligations or full-time jobs. Pell Grants could be more useful to new-stage learners if they were available to those who want to take perhaps one course per semester or earn an occupational certificate. The Higher Education Act could be modified to create "Micro Pell Grants" to meet the needs of such working learners. Similarly, the Education for Public Service Act of 2007, which provides student-loan forgiveness for those who pursue public-service work, can be modified to better meet the needs of encore adults who have returned to school to help launch social-purpose postmidlife careers. The act provides loan forgiveness for anyone who works in a 501(c)3 organization, the government, the military, law enforcement, or some other public-service role and who makes 120 consecutive monthly loan payments. Providing prorated loan forgiveness for those in the new stage would make the program more accessible to those committed to public service.

9. **An Encore Bill.** After World War II, when millions of soldiers were returning home and making the transition from military life to civilian life, we summoned our creativity in the policy realm and crafted the G.I. Bill—in part to honor their service and sacrifice and, equally, to make sure society could incorporate such a large number of people into postwar roles. Today, tens of millions going through the great midlife migration are themselves arriving at new territory in the life course. As with the returning G.I.s, their happiness and society's well-being are equally at stake. Yet there is no coherent policy agenda to help people in the new stage develop their human capital, transition into new roles, and handle the financial challenges. And there are no incentives to bring their skills to the areas where they are most needed. It's one of the reasons this shift has remained largely a do-it-yourself undertaking.

Positive signs exist, to be sure. The Troops to Teachers program, for example, shows that skills built in military careers can and do translate well to encore careers as public school teachers. Just as important, Troops to Teachers shows how this midlife juncture can offer a second chance, an opportunity not only for new fulfillment but also for social mobility, to move up the ladder in a way that wasn't possible for many when first starting out.

For Sandra Sessoms-Penny, who grew up helping her parents pick fruit in South Florida, Troops to Teachers provided an opportunity to follow her twenty-two-year U.S. Air Force career with an encore career in teaching. With the program's help, Sessoms-Penny earned a master's degree and became a social studies teacher, then an administrator at a nearby middle school, and then assistant principal of Windsor High School in Isle of Wight County, Virginia.

Bringing these measures together, along with others aimed at easing the transition (such as IPAs and LiLAs), will be critically important. It might even lead to new official structures. Just as there is a U.S. Administration on Aging, shouldn't we be considering a national administration on the new stage? Charles Handy's idea of a Third Age ministry in the EU is much the same notion.

However, the most significant step of all would be reforming Social Security in a way that makes it more aligned with the new shape of lives, while enabling it to continue to protect those who are either too sick to continue working or who want to go directly from their midlife jobs to retirement. One way this can be accomplished is for the program to become more like an annuity. Private retirement income-planning products have increasingly flexible options that enable them to be adjusted according to an individual's situation—drawing down extra benefits during career transitions or for extraordinary expenses and topping them back up when earnings are higher.

Social Security, too, can be seen as seed capital to help individuals invest in the next stage of their lives, a core asset in a lifelong financial-security portfolio. Eugene Steuerle of the Urban Institute, for example, proposes to streamline Social Security's current concoction of penalties, bonuses, and other provisions and create an open, understandable, fair, and flexible financial-services product that makes visible current incentives to work longer, such as the Delayed Retirement Credit. Such changes, he says, would incur no additional cost to the government or risk to the individual.

Another valuable innovation would be to enable individuals to stop and start their Social Security payments, as circumstances change. Individuals could begin taking Social Security at sixty-two or older, use it to subsidize renewal or a gap year, and then stop as they return to the workforce, in a way that actuarially adjusts their later payments to be revenue neutral. An even more radical approach would enable individuals to take a year or two of Social Security before sixty-two, say at fifty or fifty-five, to underwrite a transition year, with the understanding that they would begin getting full benefits later (again in an actuarially adjusted way).

These refinements in Social Security—together with initiatives to mobilize encore talent and investments in encore transitions—would send an important signal that the nation needs and values the vast assets accumulating in the encore population. Enhanced in these ways, Social Security can forge a common bond that helps people both receive essential benefits and contribute to the greater good. These measures honor the *social* in Social Security, the commitment that begins with our shared responsibility for each other. And they honor the impulse toward social purpose—helping others, giving back, making a difference, leaving a legacy—that is among the strongest motivations for working longer.

It's time to bring together a set of policy measures to enable the transition into a new stage of life, in much the way we did to ease the path to retirement. Yet we hardly have a debate about what the components of such a comprehensive Encore Bill might look like, much less any legislative momentum on this front.

10. **Get Organized.** Shifting from an outdated paradigm to a new one, from structural lag to structural lead, from that world out of whack to one in much better alignment, will not happen through vision alone. We need a social movement composed of those who have the most to gain from the change. And we'll need organizations dedicated to supporting these efforts.

There are many ways that AARP serves the interest of this group—through their publications, through much of their marketing, through helping individuals find second acts. However, a great challenge facing that organization is that it is serving all people fifty and above. Imagine an organization serving those fifty and under—as if the needs of a four-year-old and a forty-four-year-old were the same. It's difficult to lead a movement when you have so many constituencies. As a result, there is as yet no go-to organization singularly focused on advancing the new-stage agenda and cause. More positively, there are a growing number of leaders who are stepping forward to identify themselves with this stage. They've increased the visibility, the appeal, and the meaning of this period in life.

As Peter Laslett proclaimed, those in the new phase must be the ones to make this happen. However, it is a cause that all of society has an interest in, including those who will move into this period more quickly than they think.

There's no question taking these ten steps (and other promising measures) will require a sizable investment—and entail a variety of disruptions. That undeniable reality brings us squarely back to the question of benefit—and to the potential of a new map of life to transform the longevity paradox into a vast payoff.

EIGHT

The Generativity Revolution

•••••••••••••••••••••••

I met Bill Schwartz for the first time at Bay Watch, a restaurant in San Mateo, California, a small city nestled between San Francisco ten miles to the north and Silicon Valley about that distance south. No one would confuse the Bay Watch restaurant— a well-worn diner doling out inexpensive omelets and tuna sandwiches—for the television show of the same name. Nor would anybody confuse the sixtysomething Schwartz for the slick technology innovators staked out just down the peninsula.

Round, bald, and rumpled, Schwartz was a much-beloved doctor in town, a solo practitioner who started out in a different era of medicine, the kind of physician who still made house calls. Trained initially in free clinics caring for the poor and linked to teaching hospitals, he went on to become a primary-care doctor as well as an adjunct faculty member at the well-regarded University of California–San Francisco (UCSF) Medical School.

A few years earlier, while still engaged in his private practice, Schwartz started volunteering at night at Samaritan House, a local agency serving the disadvantaged. He began seeing working poor patients, those who made too much money to qualify for publicly funded medical care yet not enough to pay for health insurance. He examined them on Samaritan House's conference room table, in the makeshift doctor's office he set up in that room.

As word got around about the service and the line out the door wound down the street, Schwartz moved from one night a week to two. As demand grew further, he enlisted his friend Walter Gaines, another physician, to help out. Increment by increment, lengthening queue by lengthening queue, one buttonholed recruit after another, Schwartz's impulse to use his experience to greater effect resulted in a new community institution.

By the time I met Schwartz, he had "retired" from his own private practice, formed what had become a thriving free clinic as part of Samaritan House, recruited dozens of other Encore Stage doctors and nurses to join the cause, and turned the health center into one of the most popular rotations for young UCSF medical students and residents interested in practicing in the community, all much to his own surprise. He never thought of himself as a social entrepreneur or an entrepreneur of any kind. He was a family doctor who took care of patients.

Visiting the Samaritan House clinic was a revelation—physicians routinely spending an hour with patients, many of them children and their families, taking the time to understand the whole person and the full situation. In the hallways it was not uncommon to encounter experienced physicians and younger medical students, huddled together, engaged in a kind of two-way mentoring—the veteran docs learning about the latest developments in the field from the students and residents, the younger ones absorbing what one described to me as "the art of medicine," something they said couldn't be divined in the classroom. As Samaritan House's reputation continued to grow, staff members found themselves in the awkward position of turning away wealthier patients inquiring how they could pay top dollar to get access to medical care aimed at the poor—because in this case it was superior care.

For Schwartz, this was all a source of great pride and some bemusement. At lunch, he recounted walking past a former private practice patient on the streets of San Mateo, who recognized him, whirled around, and asked, "Didn't you used to be Dr. Schwartz?" Schwartz nodded and explained that he was still Dr. Schwartz, albeit with a different purpose and portfolio. The more I came to understand Schwartz and Samaritan House, the clearer it became that this was not another heroic transformation tale of a visionary change maker but really a classic story of new stage confluence. He was weaving together a sense of responsibility coming out of his early training in free clinics, the desire to continue to use what he learned in nearly four decades of medical practice, and the urgency to escape a phase of his career that had run its course, increasingly buffeted by insurance company constraints and malpractice fears and bereft of many of the features that had originally drawn Schwartz to medicine.

Today the Samaritan House clinic is two clinics, with nine paid staff and hundreds of pro bono doctors, nurses, and health professionals, most of them in the encore years. They handle something approaching 10,000 patient visits a year. And none of this, not the clinic or Schwartz's encore career, came out of a grand plan to transform health care in America. It was the work of an incremental, experimental (almost accidental) entrepreneur, who took a step at a time, tried to solve a problem, and brought his experience and connections to bear.

As time passed, I encountered dozens more entrepreneurs like Schwartz, women and men operating in an array of fields, all across the country, who were quietly pulling off significant accomplishments, going against the grain of societal expectation. These encounters coincided with the emergence of social entrepreneurship nationally as a prominent approach to alleviating big social problems, with new organizations like Echoing Green investing heavily in young people with big ideas and remarkable energy (Teach for America's founder, Wendy Kopp, and City Year cocreator Alan Khazei started out as Echoing Green fellows). I started thinking: This is great, but what about a vehicle to invest in innovators on the other side of midlife as well? What about Echoing *Gray*?

I began shopping the idea around to investors keen on social innovation; the rejections accumulated. Some suggested the whole project was in violation of human nature. People in their fifties, sixties, and seventies might be kindly or wizened, but innovation and entrepreneurship were, self-evidently, the domain of young people. Just look at Silicon Valley.

Then one day I got a message, essentially over the transom, from two large foundations that had been together contemplating a prize for people over sixty doing big things for the greater good. Was I interested in working with them to develop this idea? They added—graciously and aware that the prospect of money can easily distort people's interest—that I shouldn't feel any pressure to respond if this wasn't an idea that made sense.

Sometimes things just work out.

As it turns out, Sir John Templeton, the legendary investor, then well into his eighties, had been faxing messages from his home in the Bahamas to the leadership of his foundation outside of Philadelphia. What about an award—Templeton already gave out the largest cash prize in the world for outstanding contributions in religion and science—for "purpose in retirement"?

Meanwhile, The Atlantic Philanthropies, the biggest foundation backing social engagement by people in the second half of life and the largest investor in Experience Corps, had been thinking about a similar idea, interested in shifting public perception about the capacity of older people. It is probably no accident that Chuck Feeney, Atlantic's benefactor, was practicing a robust version of "purpose in retirement" himself, determined to give away the full amount of his multibillion-dollar fortune before he died (his adage: "giving while living").

Over the following months I worked with Laura Robbins from Atlantic and Kimon Sargeant from Templeton's office, and we concocted the Purpose Prize, exclusively for social innovators on the other side of midlife. The initial plan was to give out five prizes of $100,000 each year to individuals who had brought together experience, talent, and an entrepreneurial idea to help solve a major social issue facing the nation. Inverting the old mandatory-retirement equation, and eager to rebalance the scales of innovation, we (blasphemously) wouldn't even accept nominations from anyone who was *under* sixty.

I was initially euphoric about the prize's potential to change the way people view the new stage, but that excitement began to fade into anxiety just weeks away from the first nomination deadline. Already we'd been warned against giving five awards. Wouldn't a single prize help protect against the possibility that we'd throw this party and nobody would show? If we built it, would they really come?

By the first day of March 2006, when the doors closed, 1,200 nominations had been submitted. For five prizes. Each year since produced that same result. Thousands upon thousands of nominations came pouring in. Facing the opposite problem than the one originally feared, we scrambled, adding another tier of winners and fifty Purpose Prize fellows, all just to recognize the top 5 percent of nominees.

By 2009 the Purpose Prize was established, and the White House invited one of the first winners, Robert Chambers, to speak to a gathering honoring social innovators. At that event Chambers uttered a phrase that to my mind captures the essence of the prize, and the reasoning behind it: "I was old enough to recognize injustice when I saw it," he said, "and experienced enough to do something about it."

Chambers had used his earlier experience as a midlevel employee in banking, along with two years in a "retirement job" selling used cars in New Hampshire, to start Bonnie CLAC (for Car Loans and Counseling, but equally an homage to *Car Talk*'s

Click and Clack), a nonprofit aimed at helping low-income rural buyers avoid unscrupulous used-car dealers and usurious loan agents. Specifically, Bonnie CLAC helps poor people buy reliable, fuel-efficient cars at prices they can afford. Chambers understood that in rural areas a car was essential to maintain a job and that being sold an unaffordable or unreliable car was tantamount to economic homicide. As a used-car salesman, he'd seen it happen all too frequently.

Like Bill Schwartz of Samaritan House clinic, Chambers's creation was fashioned deliberately over time, through trial and error, after much rumination. This approach is reflected in the work of Inez Killingsworth, a former janitor in the Cleveland public schools and another prize winner. She initially got involved in her neighborhood trying to stop stray dogs from threatening children walking to school. That initial engagement led to fuller appreciation of the fundamental problems facing her community—and to creating an organization that today is helping thousands of poor and moderate-income people in Cleveland and other parts of Ohio to fight predatory lenders and stay in their homes.

Catalino Tapia, a winner in 2008, was a gardener just south of San Francisco, a few miles from where the Samaritan House clinic is housed. He came to the country as an illegal immigrant with six dollars in his pocket, eventually building a small gardening business. Tapia and his wife managed to put their son through UCLA and then law school at Berkeley. At his son's law school graduation, Tapia was so moved by what had been accomplished that he determined to help other parents from similar backgrounds have the same experience. To do so he created a scholarship fund focused on Latino youth, the Bay Area Gardener's Foundation. Tapia organized fellow gardeners of modest means into a grassroots philanthropy initiative that has sent dozens of students on to community college and other forms of higher education, raising money from their employers and others to pay for books, tuition, and academic support for these young people.

Jock Brandis, another winner in 2008, was a lighting guy, working on television shows and movies. He hit a bad patch, barely scraping by and taking any jobs that came his way. One Christmas, he recalls, his children purchased a book on the worst one hundred films of all time, joyfully highlighting the many that he'd had a hand in. And that, he says, was something of a high point. As his career progressed, he found himself increasingly relegated to bottom-of-the-barrel television productions—trying to make professional wrestling look authentic and Jimmy Swaggart appear honest.

Before Brandis's wife died, he went deep into debt for her cancer treatments. After she passed away, Brandis visited a friend in Mali who was serving in the Peace Corps there. He was shocked to see how harsh the peanut economy was on the hands (and wallets) of the local women who were shelling the nuts by hand, one at a time. He vowed as a thank-you to send back a mechanical device that could speed the process and ease the wear and tear on people's hands.

None existed. So, in the spirit of his former lighting trade—when someone asked you if something was possible, you always said yes, and then improvised until you figured out how to do it—Brandis invented one. His twenty-eight-dollar Universal Nut Sheller has since been distributed to villages around the world, and Brandis's organization, the Full Belly Project, is busy developing other inventions to fight global hunger and poverty. When he received his Purpose Prize, Brandis thanked the committee not only for all those who have benefited from the Universal Nut Sheller but also on behalf of his subprime lender (a second mortgage funded the project) and his dentist (who had been waiting to get paid).

THE NEW CREATIVE CLASS?

All of this might sound like reinvention mythology in another guise, but below the surface, the story of the Purpose Prize winners, for the most part, is a different one. First of all, the nominees tend to reflect a fitful, complex, and extended trajectory of achievement, one in which their innovations are less a departure from past work and more a bringing together of elements gathered over time, building upon previous work, using old skills in new ways to often dramatic effect. And frequently they are tales that run against the common glossy-magazine narrative of success to significance, of ex-presidents and ex-CEOs who go on to new glory. More often, like Brandis's story, they reflect resilience and redemption, going *from setback to significance*. It's a message that second chances can come with longer lives, that there's time to learn life's lessons, face some ups and downs, and redirect in a way that can bring greater contribution and meaning.

Most of all, to me, the story of the Purpose Prize is about upending conventional wisdom, beginning most obviously with the idea that an older nation means an inevitable period of declining innovation, entrepreneurship, and creativity. That's just the way it works, the dictum goes. Phillip Longman, author of *The Empty Cradle* and a fellow at the New America Foundation, warns, "After the proportion of elders increases in a society beyond a certain point, the level of entrepreneurship and inventiveness decreases."

As it turns out, and as the Purpose Prize reveals, there's reason to believe that conventional wisdom on this subject is more conventional than wise. As *Newsweek* reported in an August 2010 article, "The Golden Age of Innovation," the locus of entrepreneurship in America has shifted to the fifty-five-to-sixty-four age group. Individuals over fifty-five are nearly twice as likely to create successful companies as their counterparts in the twenty-to-thirty-four age group.

But the definitive understanding of the phenomenon of late-blooming creativity comes from University of Chicago economist David Galenson. Through years of research, first on painters and then on poets, songwriters, film directors, and other artists and innovators, Galenson has been able to show that genius clusters into two categories. Conceptual geniuses tend to do their best work while young, producing breakthrough ideas early in their careers. By contrast, experimental geniuses bloom late. In Galenson's formulation, this breakdown is not a function of age but of creative style and time. Whereas conceptual geniuses work out their ideas in advance, oftentimes in their heads, experimental geniuses by their very nature need a long period of time to reach their peak, moving forward by trial and error, slowly accumulating the elements that will be integrated in their fully realized work.

Galenson points to Picasso as an example of conceptual genius. He did his most important paintings, as measured by their market value, by his midtwenties. Picasso's early paintings were worth approximately four times the value of the work he did in his sixties. Cézanne exemplifies experimental brilliance. Cézanne's paintings created in his sixties sold for fifteen times the value of his paintings as a young artist.

Galenson goes on to observe that in our day and age, "We are conditioned to believe that the only innovative people who make important contributions to our culture and economy are whiz kids fresh from prestigious art schools and institutes of technology, who leap to sudden, dramatic discoveries and quickly become rich and famous." There's no denying the essential value of brilliant young people, and the contributions of young people in general. But experimental genius, present in men and women "who spend decades gaining experience and knowledge," is also critically important—and that potential is often obscured or, worse, truncated. Yet it is all around us, steadily percolating in unexpected places. We may pass these late bloomers on the street or, as Galenson suggests, "see them when we look in the mirror."

Malcolm Gladwell, distilling Galenson's work, argues that we need to make room at the table for the Picassos and the Cézannes of the world, for youthful prodigy *and* late-blooming creativity. To illustrate his point in a particularly boomer context, he contrasts the trajectories of Fleetwood Mac and the Eagles. In Gladwell's telling, the Eagles are cut from the cloth of conceptual genius—they find their sound right away, their inaugural album is a gold record, their third record is a greatest-hits compilation, followed by their creative peak, *Hotel California*. All in four years. "They go from zero to sixty," Gladwell remarks. "They hit their absolute apotheosis."

Not so with Fleetwood Mac. They bounce around for years, going through incarnation after incarnation, experimenting with blues, party music, reggae, instrumentals, producing one mediocre album after another, changing personnel regularly, until they finally find their footing. Their fifteenth album sells more than 4 million copies, and their sixteenth album, *Rumours*, sells 19 million copies—making it, at the time, the greatest-selling rock album in history. By the time the band Fleetwood Mac reaches its peak, Gladwell continues, "the band's original members are literally onto their third marriage. They have kids in high school. Their hair is gray. They have IRAs."

The point is that there are multiple styles of creativity, the Eagles and Fleetwood Mac, Picasso and Cézanne. The problem is, Gladwell concludes—excepting some high-profile counterexamples—"for some reason in our accounting of genius and creativity, we have forgotten to make sense of the Cézanne's of the world." And that brings with it both hope for the future and a kind of sadness. How many people with the potential to do their best work late but without iron-willed persistence have been discouraged, written off because their promise failed to manifest itself early, assumed to be over the hill after their previous efforts failed—when, in truth, they were just getting started, preparing to ascend that hill?

In the words of Mihaly Csikszentmihalyi, author of *Flow* and a professor at Claremont Graduate University, "Do we know how many geniuses are never recognized because their talents are blighted before they have a chance to be expressed? The fact is, nobody does."

THE ABUNDANCY RATIO

I don't want to create the false impression that everyone in the new stage is going to become Cézanne, or for that matter Inez Killingsworth. To me the lesson is this: If we are going to break free from limited and limiting conventional wisdom, starting with misconceptions about the distribution of creativity, entrepreneurship, and innovation across the life course, let's finish the job. Why not rid ourselves of all the accepted orthodoxy that misunderstands the prospects of longevity and inhibits our ability to make the most of this opportunity?

Let's start by jettisoning slogans like "working-age population" (code for those under sixty with something to contribute), "elder share" (meaning countries mired in people over sixty), and "dependency ratio" (quite simply, too many old people, defined as sixty and above). These phrases are treated as immutable fact yet really amount to utterly arbitrary conceptions, usually plagued by a cramped zero-sum logic. The ideas, as Peter Laslett commented, mark the persistence into the present of notions belonging wholly to the past. Scenario planning through the rearview mirror.

There's a place for sustainability. But there are some notions that should simply be discarded, like these code words for a demographically determined, rapidly approaching collapse. They continue to flow steadily from a set of apocalyptic articles and books, tragic tales that seem to garner more attention and greater credibility the gloomier their predictions. In front of me sits the November 2010 issue of *Foreign Policy*. Apparently not to be outdone by *Foreign Affairs'* "aging pains" article earlier this year, the *Foreign Policy* cover depicts three elderly Asian women, grimly planted on a park bench under the bold, capitalized cover headline, "OLD WORLD." The feature article describes the "gray tsunami" that is "sweeping the planet," a "population bomb" of old people (one wonders whether the Weather Channel or FEMA is sponsoring these pieces—which invariably invoke fiscal hurricanes, tidal waves of decripitude, and an agequake or two to convey the notion that something catastrophic is about to take place). The article goes on to inform readers, "The faster evolving and more technologically sophisticated a society becomes, the more rapidly job skills—and elderly workers, sadly—become obsolete."

A variation on this point of view is echoed in a recent piece by University of Texas economist James Galbraith as part of an *Atlantic* debate on boomers, the aging society, and the fiscal situation. Galbraith—a boomer himself—opines that "worn-out boomers" should go immediately to the sidelines, without passing go: "Get out of the workforce. Give up your jobs so that ambitious, harder-working and more capable young people can have them. Go home and enjoy life." (Columnist Ellen Goodman observes that we castigate those over sixty, on the one hand, for sitting on their butts and lapping up leisure and, on the other hand, for staying in the contributing workforce and foreclosing opportunities for others.)

This woeful picture is rapidly becoming orthodoxy in the media. Beyond the catchphrases, the story runs something like this: America (and much of the developed world) is hurtling toward a situation in which tens of millions of people, arguably the single biggest group in society, and a mighty political force to boot, are about to dominate the scene. At somewhere around age sixty, they will, pretty much overnight, become the elderly, pass out of the "working-age population," become incompetent and incontinent, bankrupt the health care system, vote for hefty increases in public spending on their retirement at the expense of everyone else, turn the Sun Belt into a giant golf course, and ignite a war that will, in the subtitle of the 2010 book *Shock of Gray*, pit "Young Against Old, Child Against Parent, Worker Against Boss, Company Against Rival, and Nation Against Nation." What about Motherhood Against Apple Pie? Now that's a world out of whack. It's a disaster movie—*Return of the Codger*, *Invasion of the Budget Snatchers*, *The Age Blob*.

To be sure, there is the real prospect that things might not work out so well if we don't rise up to the new realities, take on genuine challenges, and embrace fresh possibilities. In my view, the more worrisome dystopian scenario is characterized by a sense of awkward muddle and missed opportunity, a nation in which the largest segment of society is at loose ends and under-engaged—consigned to a kind of identity oblivion, fighting age discrimination, facing foreclosed opportunities, mired in personal stagnation, and bereft of purpose. If that happens, we'll squander the most experienced segment of the population after investing countless resources in their human capital, at a time when we need much of what they have to offer. Gone also will be the tax revenues and health gains that accompany longer contributing and engaged lives. There might in fact be growing generational tension if individuals are cast aside, relegated to age-segregated living arrangements, pushed to pursue a second childhood, deprived of a broader worldview, and encouraged to vote their narrow interests.

In this book I have attempted to outline a different prospect, one in which the invention of a new stage between midlife and true old age anchors a revamped vision of the life course, a fresh map tailored to the life spans and possibilities of the present and the future. The Encore Stage, in fully realized form, is characterized by confluence over reinvention, by the weaving together of accumulated skills, insights, perspective, and experiences into a new amalgam. It is epitomized by encore careers that provide continued income, new meaning, and social impact, and can be enhanced greatly by pathways and policies that promote social mobility and cross-generational connection. The end result promises to be a windfall of talent for society unlike anything we've seen since women moved into new productive roles in the 1960s and 1970s.

Of course, back then there was also much consternation—about how these women were going to displace men in a zero-sum logic that sounds an awful lot like contemporary worries that longer contributing lives will necessarily come at the expense of young people. Human rights aside, today we couldn't conceive of losing the talent that women represent, of banishing half the productive labor force and still competing internationally. I predict several decades down the road we'll have a similar perspective on the contribution by those in the encore years, women and men alike. We'll wonder how we ever survived before these groups came to play critical roles in society. Comments about the incompetence of these individuals, like some of those above, will come to be regarded in much the way pronouncements of segregationist governors or male chauvinists from a bygone era are seen today.

Ultimately, if we can rid ourselves of the anachronistic thinking that holds back individual lives and society more broadly, if we mount the social construction project that new life stages require and build a social movement not just of encore adults but younger generations who themselves stand to gain much through the creation of this new phase of life, we might bring on an unanticipated abundance where others have posited only deficits and decay.

When it comes to advancing economic innovation and tackling societal problems, one often wonders—wistfully in these days of tight budgets—"What if money were no object? What would be possible?" Well, what if talent were no object? What if we made full use of the vast stores of human and social capital built up in the encore population? We might break through to entirely new opportunities for economic growth and social progress.

We might even be able to replace the tyranny of dependency ratios and other symbols of foreclosed possibility with something quite the opposite. How about an abundancy ratio? Experience plus perspective plus motivation plus time, multiplied by demography, leveraged by new institutions and policies and markets, realized not only in the coming years but for generations to come, equals a society that makes sense again. Now that's a ratio worth embracing.

An abundancy ratio is also the core of a new sustainability, one that refuses to throw away human beings before they are used up just as steadfastly as it is unwilling to waste paper or plastic. And that's not only sustainable, it's attainable. We invented retirement out of thin air a half century ago, and youth a half century before that, in each case to turn a problem into a solution. Today, it is time to take on the social construction project that is the Encore Stage of life, to finish the story of longer life courses, to change the shape of lives from one tailored for a century past to one designed for the years ahead. It is a time to create the "Indian summer" G. Stanley Hall articulated, in place of the long, gray winter so widely assumed today.

THE GENERATIVITY REVOLUTION

Of all the benefits to be realized through creating a new stage, the biggest prize of all may be a cultural transformation to accompany the talent revolution described above. We could produce what columnist David Brooks calls a Generativity Revolution.

Many are concerned today, across the political spectrum, that we are disregarding our future, leaving matters worse for coming generations environmentally, educationally, financially, and in myriad other ways. Bill Clinton made this observation in 2010, contending that we need to once again become a "tomorrow society," to get back into "the future business." There is growing worry that we have lost that powerful instinct as a nation, that we have gotten off track, that we face a new kind of deficit, a *posterity* deficit. There's fear that we've lost the fundamental value of generativity, the recognition and appreciation that we're a species that must confront mortality and that by its very nature has to tend to the well-being of future generations to survive.

In a conversation with writer Daniel Goleman in 1988, Erik Erikson himself registered this concern. Eighty-six at the time, he warned that we were on the verge of losing generativity as a cultural value. "The only thing that can save us as a species," he said, "is seeing how we're not thinking about future generations in the way we live. What's lacking is generativity, a generativity that will promote positive values in the lives of the next generation."

Our continuing addiction to prolonging our own youth—the futile attempt to fool ourselves and others that we are younger than we are, what Betty Friedan calls "the youth short circuit"—remains a central part of this problem that Erikson describes. This folly is reflected in the immortality quest, one both quixotic and disturbing. Leon Kass, an ethics scholar at the University of Chicago, characterizes this outlook as the "childish desire to eat one's life and keep it too," a narcissism that is "incompatible with devotion to posterity." He adds that this perspective is "in principle hostile to children, because children, those who come after, are those who will take one's place; *they* are life's answer to mortality."

Indeed, we seem to have lost the essence of *the human project* centered on the generative impulse to pass on life's lessons to future generations. As Harvard Medical School scholar George Vaillant argues, "Biology flows downhill." It is human nature to focus on the well-being of future generations. That's part of true maturity, of accepting limits. We're also endangering the parallel impulse, what might be called *the American project*, the responsibility to make things better for future generations. That has always been the immigrant dream for America. It is a cornerstone of the American Dream, the belief that one's children should have it better than we do.

More recently, these concerns have reached a new urgency. One poll by AARP found that Americans in the second half of life worry that they will be the first generation in American history to leave things worse off for the next generation. Another poll shows that boomers in particular hold this view. Beyond surveys, this theme has become a thread in commencement addresses. One *Wall Street Journal* headline from 2009 highlights the phenomenon: "Boomers to This Year's Grads: We Are Really, Really Sorry . . . "

Those in the encore years constitute our great national repository of generativity, a renewable resource of caring for the future. This group is poised to answer Erikson's challenge. For some time, we've thwarted the expression of this impulse, sending people in their sixties, seventies, and beyond—arguably our generative heartland—to age-segregated leisure villages, consigning them to live out a pale approximation of a second childhood, free from the prospect of paying school taxes or being disturbed by the patter of little feet.

The new stage is about putting that notion of a second childhood aside. It's about being a grown-up, about breaking once and for all our addiction to youth. Instead of succumbing to fantasies of an endless childhood, we need to embrace our stage and the generative impulse that's such an important part of real maturity. *Instead of trying to be younger than we are, we need to accept our age and our stage and invest in those who truly are young*—who represent the future. Rather than trying to *be* them, we need to *be there* for them, to support their development and well-being so that they can carry the dream forward.

Life stages are not just social construction projects; they are social reflection projects. The notion of adolescence was created not just to solve a problem but also to reflect our identity—the identity of a youthful nation and all the hopes and the dreams that went with that conception. Today we have to stop pretending, or wishing, we're the same country we were in 1904 when the sixty-year-old G. Stanley Hall invented the category of adolescence. We're a nation that will soon have more older people than younger ones—indeed, part of a developed world that is expected by 2050 to have twice as many people over sixty as under fifteen. Let's face it: We're rapidly on the way to becoming an older nation, like it or not. We can spend our time lamenting that we're no longer what we once were demographically. Or we can truly accept the responsibility that comes with being in the Encore Stage, which is most of all the generative mantle.

In this way, creating and embracing the new stage can be for a grown-up nation what the invention and embrace of youth were for an adolescent America—a kind of touchstone, a reflection of our new, and true, identity, a centerpiece of a contemporary version of the American Dream, one that aligns the new life spans with a life course designed to make the most of it.

CALLING GENERATION E

The question of what we owe future generations was very much in the air in a packed hall at Stanford the night the 2009 Purpose Prizes were awarded, as was the question of mortality. Among the winners that night were Elizabeth and Stephen Alderman, by their own description an ordinary suburban couple living outside New York whose lives were transformed when their son Peter was killed attending a conference in the World Trade Center on September 11.

The Aldermans struggled with how to respond. They thought about building a playground in his name or creating a scholarship. Then one night, fighting insomnia, Elizabeth Alderman saw a *Nightline* special on the victims of posttraumatic stress in war zones around the world. Nearly a billion people, a sixth of the world's population, were suffering from these aftereffects.

She and her husband were eager to do something to show that their son Peter had lived, that his life had made a difference and would continue to do so. Without a thought to the label *social entrepreneur*, they began to form alliances with groups like Paul Farmer's Partners in Health to create mental health services where none had ever existed. Nearly a decade later, their clinics have served more than 100,000 people in Rwanda, Uganda, Cambodia, and elsewhere.

The same evening Elizabeth and Stephen Alderman received their Purpose Prize, an honorary posthumous award was given to Ken Bacon, a former *Wall Street Journal* editor who took a leave from journalism to serve as a spokesman for the Defense Department in the 1990s. Bacon's experience in that role changed his outlook profoundly. It led him away from the news-paper world and into a new role as head of Refugees International, an organization dedicated to advocating for displaced persons and promoting solutions to displacement crises. He distinguished himself in that encore career before being diagnosed with melanoma. He was treated, but it was too late—the cancer was already spreading through his bloodstream. A year and a half after a malignant lesion was removed, a tumor was discovered in Bacon's brain.

Just a few months after he died, Bacon's wife, Darcy, accepted the honorary Purpose Prize for her husband. She described Ken Bacon's final weeks, days, and hours. They were a vivid concentration of purpose. As he put his affairs in order, he focused on two things: the people he loved, spending much of his final allotment of time with his wife, children, family, and friends, and the cause to which he was dedicated, the plight of refugees, especially what he viewed as the great issue of the future—refugees from climate change. In between firing off letters to the *New York Times* protesting the army's inadequate efforts at suicide prevention and an opinion piece published in the *Washington Post* on how we could improve health care in America from the perspective of someone dying of cancer, Bacon set up a center at Refugees International focused on climate change—spending precious final days and hours linked to something beyond himself, beyond his life, to the well-being of future generations.

In her remarks to the Purpose Prize gathering, Darcy Bacon recalled that shortly before the end, she and her husband went to a house on the Rhode Island coast and listened to music that they had sung together in a small church choir, Mozart's *Missa*

Brevis. Bacon confided in her, "I hope my life won't be a *missa brevis.*" He died a few days later.

Many of us who left Stanford that night felt especially grateful to be healthy and alive, more determined to make the most of the time ahead, hopeful that our own lives added up to more than a *missa brevis.*

As individuals, it's hard for any of us who have moved beyond our fiftieth birthday to know how much time we have to do what needs to be done. For me, with three small children, I hope it is a long time indeed. And I hope to spend it not only helping to nurture our own little generativity revolution at home but also realizing the prospect that this book has attempted to articulate— to carry out the lessons that I have learned from Peter Laslett and Meredith McKenzie and so many others who are inventing the future through their ideas and deeds, "one river at a time."

As a generation, we have been granted what amounts to a great gift of time—of experience, understanding, and the capacity to do something with it. We have the chance to transform the shape of lives, to build something beautiful, to bequeath to younger generations a fertile stage where once sat a kind of chasm.

Therein also lies some generational redemption. Instead of going out as Generation B (for lack of anything better) or "the grayest generation" (as some have dubbed us)—a cohort in danger of being remembered more for its size and dates of birth than anything else—we can forge a new identity based on what we've accomplished and what we've passed on. We can leave the stage as Generation E, having made the most of our encore.

Each generation has its task, its opportunity, its moment of truth. Let us be remembered for what survives of us, for living our legacy, for leaving the world a better place than we found it.

ACKNOWLEDGMENTS

I've incurred a considerable debt in the research and writing of this book, beginning with all the time, ideas, and openness contributed by the new-stage pioneers at the heart of this project. Vast thanks go to all those who were interviewed and who gave so much of themselves to the project. My only regret is that not everyone could be included in the final product, even though their insights are reflected throughout.

Stefanie Weiss, Civic Ventures's gifted communications guru, helped immensely with ideas, edits, and impetus, as did the inimitable John Gomperts, who continued to offer astute guidance even as he left Civic Ventures to lead the AmeriCorps program. Jenny Griffin provided invaluable help with interviews, research, and suggestions, as did Ruchira Shah, who helped uncover the history of the new-stage idea. I am grateful as well to Civic Ventures colleagues Marci Alboher, David Bank, Phyllis Segal, and Jim Emerman, who read and commented on various drafts. Cal Halvorsen contributed valuable research on education for the second half of life. Michele Melendez provided essential edits and feedback. Vanessa Alabarces, Doug Braley, Jennifer Coate, David Cohen, Judy Goggin, Lyle Hurst, Michelle Hynes, Alexandra Kent, Leslye Louie, Janet Luce, Sarah Maple, Terry Nagel, Nancy Peterson, Carol Rudisill, and Richard Smith all helped in various and important ways. As always, the Civic Ventures board—led by Ruth Wooden and Mike Bailin—contributed substantively while providing unfailing support.

I am enormously grateful to the heroic efforts of a number of friends and colleagues who provided wise counsel and emotional succor, either directly or through their inspirational work, or both. Vast thanks go to Lincoln Caplan and David Bornstein for their commentary and guidance on the manuscript—if only I'd been able to realize their wise suggestions! Appreciation goes as well to a set of individuals who provided inspiration and counsel all along the way, including Andy Achenbaum, Mary Catherine Bateson, Geraldine Bedell, Bill Berkeley, Ann Bowers, Laura Carstensen, Michael Chodos, Barbara Dillon, Stacey Easterling, Chris Farrell, Lew Feldstein, Andy Goodman, Ellen Goodman, Sally Greengross, Alex Harris, Donna Stone Hellenbrand, Yvonne Hunt, Rosabeth Moss Kanter, Gara LaMarche, Sherry Lansing, Carol Larson, Sara Lawrence-Lightfoot, Charlie Leadbeater, Suzanne Braun Levine, Jane Lowe, Webb McKinney, Phyllis Moen, Tom Nelson, Sally Osberg, Dan Pink, Bob Putnam, Laura Robbins, Tom Rosenstiel, Jack Rosenthal, Beverly Ryder, Kimon Sargeant, Ellen Schall, Fritz Schwarz, Ed Speedling, Donna Stone, Pamela Thompson, Anthea Tinker, Cathy Ventura-Merkel, Gary Walker, and Andrew Yarrow.

I want to give particular thanks to Jan Hively, founder of the organization SHiFT, which inspired the title for this book. Likewise, I want to express my gratitude to Steve McConnell and John Rother, who organized an innovative workshop and retreat at Ghost Ranch that taught me how important new life-transition approaches could be.

It was a privilege and a pleasure to work once again with Robert Kimzey at PublicAffairs, editor extraordinaire, and with Susan Weinberg, who offered exceptional guidance through several incarnations of this project. Peter Osnos, mentor, friend, trusted adviser, and the abiding force behind PublicAffairs, helped at every turn—as he did with *Encore* and *Prime Time*. It has been a great privilege to be part of the PublicAffairs family.

I owe a deep debt intellectually to the following: Peter Laslett, who showed me great kindness a decade and a half ago; Sara Lawrence-Lightfoot, whose book *The Third Chapter*, much like Mary Catherine Bateson's *Composing a Further Life* and Laura Carstensen's *A Long Bright Future*, served as an intellectual basis for this project; and the late John W. Gardner, whose friendship and thinking have informed everything I have done since meeting him.

This book benefited from support financially and in every other way from The Atlantic Philanthropies, the David and Lucile Packard Foundation, the John Templeton Foundation, the Skoll Foundation, the Hunt Alternatives Fund, and MetLife Foundation.

My wife, Leslie Gray, deserves a medal for putting up with me during the extended process of writing this book, as do our three children, Gabriel, Levi, and Micah, who had to share their early years with a greedy sibling, this volume. Leslie juggled three children under five; a husband constantly distracted, anguished, or on the road; yet still managed to provide unfailing emotional support (along with pithy comments on the manuscript). To my entire family I want to say: I am eternally grateful, for your patience and generosity, but most of all your love. Without you, this book would not exist.

APPENDIX

Eight Stories from the Next Stage

The eight first-person accounts included in the Appendix are based on many interviews with the individuals featured. They have been condensed into a narrative form and edited for clarity. The interviews were conducted primarily during 2009 and 2010.

THEN; NOW

Cindy Moeller
Minneapolis, Minnesota

I was in my late twenties, being interviewed for a scholarship at the Kellogg Graduate School of Management at Northwestern. The interviewer looked at my record—undergraduate degree in sociology and education, MSW, four years as a social worker in public schools—and said, "This is an interesting change you're about to make from social work to business. You know that the business world is primarily about making money, and some part of you is obviously about making a difference. How are you going to feed that part of you while working in the business world?"

It was a brilliant question, and I've thought about it many times since. At the time, I spoke from the heart, and it was the truth, although I had never thought about it until that very moment. I said, "Well, you know, I'll find various things to get involved in, volunteering, being on boards, things like that, and later in my career I will probably get back into nonprofit work, or education, or something like that."

I never had any plan. I never had an age in mind. I never had any specific idea of what I was going to do. I just always had this intention in the back of my mind.

She must have liked my answer because I got the scholarship and I got my MBA, and I worked in human resources for a variety of corporations and high-tech companies in the Midwest and in Silicon Valley for twenty-some years. And then, when I was fifty-two, my mom got sick and passed away, and that was really a life-altering moment for me. I thought, "What am I doing?" I didn't have any reason to think I wouldn't be around for a while, but I thought, "Life is short, and if you're going to do something different, you need to do it." I felt this great sense of urgency. I had the same conversation with myself over and over. I thought, "Cindy, you know, 'later in your career,' that really is now. Are you serious about the stuff you've been saying to yourself for more than twenty years now?"

Losing my mom made me realize that life is finite and you have to take action to do the things that you value and think are important. I knew that if I wanted to make a serious contribution doing something else, using whatever skills and talents and expertise I have now, then I didn't want to wait until I was sixty or sixty-five and really retired to do it. I wanted to do it at a time when I could have a longer stretch of time to really make a difference.

Education appealed to me, and I stumbled on the New Leaders for New Schools program on the Internet. New Leaders runs an intensive yearlong program to train people from other fields to become school principals. I thought it sounded absolutely perfect.

Four months after my mother died, I took the plunge, joined New Leaders for New Schools, and moved back to Chicago. I spent the summer in their training program in Washington, D.C., and then did a principal residency at a Chicago public school, which unfortunately wasn't what I expected it to be. I shadowed a principal who, over six years, had moved his school from 21 percent of the kids proficient at grade level to 29 percent. And that is great, but what about the other 71 percent who are behind, who aren't proficient at grade level?

There were other problems that I did not expect as well. I expected that I would be able to become a principal in a Chicago public school, but I was told halfway through my resident year by knowledgeable people that principals in Chicago are picked by elected people in the neighborhoods around each school and that the likelihood of someone with a background like mine getting one of those jobs was very small. I finished the program and sent out résumés, but I never got a single interview to be a principal.

After months of networking, I landed a job as director of a new charter school in Minnesota. When I started in April, the board had a charter and some grant funds and a lot of really good things in place, but they had only ten students for the coming fall and no building. We worked like maniacs for about six weeks, and by June 1 we had twenty students and the prospect of a mediocre building. As a businessperson, I just didn't see how we were going to attract enough students, like seventy or eighty more, to be financially sustainable in the fall. And I just thought, like, "What the hell are we really doing here?"

Eventually, the board and I decided to defer our opening for a year and regroup so we could get off to a stronger start. We looked at a lot of different things—location, curriculum, marketing strategies. A supporter suggested that there might be a fair amount of interest in the Twin Cities in a school with a focus on Chinese language and culture. For reasons that I absolutely cannot explain, I just fell in love with the idea. And even though I kept researching all the other things that the board and I agreed on, I was really working especially hard on the Chinese idea. The board was interested but skeptical. They asked me to find at least twenty-five parents who were truly interested in the idea and several new board members with a Chinese connection.

I started putting up notices in public libraries and scheduling public meetings, and somehow I got connected to the adoptive community and they helped spread the word. One day I Googled *Chinese teacher* and *Minnesota* and found Margaret Wong, a well-established Chinese teacher who connected me to possible board members. And it just started to jell. She became one of the founding board members of Yinghua.

I felt like I was on a mission to start Yinghua. I knew it was a winner of an idea, and I was very determined to make it work. We opened the Yinghua Academy in September 2006 with 76 students in grades K–3. We started our fifth year of operation in the fall of 2010 as a K–7 school with 380 students. Yinghua Academy is the first Chinese immersion charter public school in the United States and the first Chinese immersion school in the Midwest.

I've been chair of the board the entire time—it's been an unpaid, part-time labor of love for me. Anytime I'm there, I just pinch myself. Opening Yinghua is one of the greatest achievements of my life.

Cindy Moeller lives in St. Paul, Minnesota. Over the past five years, she's supported herself leading various projects at the Center for School Change, the Minnesota Council on Foundations, and Charter School Partners. She continues to serve on the Yinghua Academy board and is now working as the part-time start-up director of Pierre Bottineau French Immersion, a new self-governed school in the Minneapolis school district.

THEN; NOW

Michael Burke
Baltimore, Maryland

I was beginning to hit seventeen, eighteen years of cooking. When you cook, you tend to work prime time. You're working Sundays, you're working weekends, you're working nights, you're standing up all day, and I was realizing that this was just too much for me. My arthritis began to get bad, and I just couldn't take it, you know.

So I called my pastor at my church, and I told her what was going on. She said, "Michael, why don't you just come here and work in the soup kitchen and do some things around the church for a while until you can figure out what you want to do? We'll take care of you."

I worked at my church, Ames Memorial United Methodist, as a building facilitator. I did some cooking in the soup kitchen and in summer camps for the children. I started working with the little children. I was having fun with the kids and started doing some of the children's sermons. I sometimes showed them how to do art because I'm a painter. An AmeriCorps alumnus said, "Michael, you're really doing good work with those kids. There's a program called Experience Corps. You should try that." I said, "I don't know. I've been working in kitchens and cussing and yelling. I don't think I can work with a child in a school." Truthfully, I was frightened by the idea of going into an elementary school. I had begun to lose my teeth, so I was self-conscious. I said, "This isn't going to work. I'm not going to school looking like this." I was worried about how the kids would look at me. When I got there, they asked, "Where are your teeth, Mr. Burke? What happened to you?"

I felt intimidated because I didn't know if the children were going to like me. I kept thinking I would get upset one day and start yelling at them. I really did. I didn't know what was going to happen. But those kids actually changed me for the better.

I was at an elementary school in Dallas, and it was just so beautiful. And the children, oh, wow! Next thing you know, I'm this guy that people are looking at, you know, just totally different now. I'm not thinking of myself anymore. Next thing you know, I said, "Let me get myself together."

I remember an experience I had with one child. It was Martin Luther King's birthday, and I wanted him to draw something. He was acting up, and he was saying, "Why should I care about him getting shot? My uncle got shot, so-and-so got shot. I don't care."

I said, "Well, let's just write his name there."

He said, "I don't even know how to spell."

I said, "I tell you what, I'm going to teach you how to spell. We're going to write down 'Happy Birthday' to Martin Luther King—that's all you've got to do. The first thing we're going to do is we're going to put down an *H*."

He said, "I don't know how to do an *H*."

So I said, "I'm going to show you how you write an *H*." So I went down and wrote down the letter *T*. I said, "There you go, there's the *H*."

He said, "That's not an *H*."

I said, "That's a different *H*."

He said, "That's not an *H*."

I said, "How are you going to tell me? I'm grown. I know what the letters are. This is an *H*."

He said, "No, it's a *T*. This is how you make an *H*."

We went through the whole scenario like that. It became a game. After a while, he wrote, "Happy Birthday," and everybody said, "Michael, how did you do that?" So I realized that I was a good person with children, that I had a lot inside of me that children needed. They weren't getting certain little things. I said, "This is wonderful." And it's been that way. It's just been a wonderful experience.

I wrote a diary about my time in the school, and at the end of the year, I went to the principal, and I said, "Look, I want you to see something." I sat down and I read her parts of the thing, and she busted out crying. And then we both started crying.

But at the beginning, I was so afraid. When you do something for a very, very long time—it's like if you're a teacher and you taught for a very long time and then you retire, and then someone wants you to come and volunteer. You have to put that teacher, that authoritative teacher, away. You have to start all over. And I had to put parts of me away.

It was hard sometimes to walk into some place and just humble yourself and have somebody say, "Well, what you need to do is this and that." And a side of you wants to say, "Look, I'm fifty-plus years old. I know how to do that. You don't have to tell me." It's good to know things, but you don't want to use your experience like that, as if "I'm just a know-it-all; you can't tell me anything." You're supposed to humble yourself and be resourceful, so people can say, "You know what? Every time I go to Michael, he has some pretty good answers. He's all right."

So, I had to humble myself. The children helped me, because when you're working with children, you have to kind of humble yourself. You have to speak well and softly. You have to look them in the eye. If you want them to listen to you, you have to be authentic, you know?

As an Experience Corps tutor for fifteen hours each week, Michael Burke received small stipends from the federally funded AmeriCorps program. At the same time, he took an office technology course and computer classes at the Community College of Baltimore County. After Burke spent three years as a tutor, Experience Corps in Baltimore hired him as a program assistant and training coordinator. He also continues to volunteer as a mentor of a nine-year-old boy with the Building Futures program at the Y of Central Maryland in Baltimore.

THEN; NOW

James Otieno
San Jose, California

I always told my wife that I was going to retire early. In fact, I was joking with her and told her I was going to retire at thirty-five. Then I amended my plans and told her I was going to retire at forty-five. As it turned out, I missed my target by two years—a complete failure! I retired at forty-seven.

The reason I wanted to retire early was to do something good for society—to give back to my native Kenya. I was born in Kisumu, a city near Lake Victoria. I came to the United States when I was eleven with my mother and two brothers. My father was already here, part of a contingent of Kenyans who came here for an exchange program for aspiring individuals in Africa—the same contingent, as it turns out, that President Obama's father was part of.

I went to the University of Minnesota and graduated with a degree in economics and psychology and then got a master's in industrial relations. A number of companies came calling, and I decided to go the corporate route. I took a job with Hewlett-Packard (HP) because the environment was very conducive to learning, and the people there were very genuine. They asked me where I'd like to spend my first few years, and I chose compensation and human resources (HR). Lo and behold, they gave me good assignments right away.

At the beginning, like a typical new MBA, I thought I'd stay in the company a few years and then move on to something else, to greener pastures to build my wealth. But, as it turned out, twenty-four years later, I was still there. I learned a lot, engaged a lot, had great assignments, great people to work with, and that's why I stayed.

By the time I retired, I was the vice president of executive compensation and services for the company. I managed a compensation portfolio of about a billion dollars, with 3,000-plus executives that I provided guidance to on a worldwide basis. I felt that I had done everything I'd been meaning to do in the corporate world, particularly in my profession. I was ready to change careers.

First, I wanted to take some time off—about a year to recalibrate. Right after I retired, I had cervical fusion surgery, so I needed four or five months just to recover. Toward the end of my year, HP called me and said, "Hey, we've got this new Encore Fellowships program with Civic Ventures and the Packard Foundation, and we thought you might be interested in helping us to pilot it." And I said, "Huh? You've got a program that places recent retirees in nonprofits in Silicon Valley where we take on significant, part-time, yearlong assignments; help the non-profit advance; and learn something about the nonprofit sector? Wow! That sounds good. Count me in!"

I chose to work with the Silicon Valley Education Foundation. They wanted to focus on human resource issues initially, and then they needed some help in finance and board governance. I thought that was a good match and said, "Let's make a go of it." And so that's what happened.

My first assignment was with HR, which I thought was going to take the full year, but in three weeks, I'd worked with the process, written a whole analysis and report to the board, and outsourced HR. Then I moved on to describe the financial structure and recruit a financial person to come in-house, who then was eventually able to put a process in place. And then I worked on board governance–related issues. We're still working on that. Then I was asked to help with strategy—that was a great entryway to the organization, because, in order to work on strategy, you have to talk to everybody, which is great. I had a blast.

And I learned a lot. A number of fellows in my group grew up in a world where at some point in our careers, we pretty much got a lot of things that we wanted, and we had a lot of resources, and we morphed into fairly aggressive creatures, thinking that we can do everything and we can own the world. Our patience is very thin, and we want things done very fast, and we think we know the formula to get it done right.

But we have to be careful. If you go into the nonprofit sector saying, "I know how to do this. I know how to fix this because I've done it be-fore," it's a losing proposition. We have to go in with, "Yes, I have certain skill sets that have not been deployed in this sector. I have certain learn-ings from the for-profit sector. But I also have something to learn about the nonprofit environment, and I have to see how I can balance the skill sets that I have and bring them into this environment in a more collaborative manner, rather than a forceful, aggressive manner." And I think that is what the program is doing.

After I finished my fellowship, I agreed to stay on and see the strategy work through on a part-time basis. And you know what part time means—forty hours a week instead of seventy. It's a challenge fitting in everything I'm trying to do. I started a foundation called the Karibu Rafiki Foundation, which means "Welcome Friend" in Swahili. We focus on the underserved women and children of Kenya and Sudan—providing financial support, building schools, whatever it takes. And on top of that, I'm the chair of the board of Palo Alto University and serve on the board of the Children's Health Council and the Child Advocates of Silicon Valley, where we train volunteers to work with kids in the foster-care system.

I have no moments of doubt, no regrets. Even though I seem to be doing quite a bit now, it's nowhere close to what I was doing before. Well, I do have one regret—I still don't have enough time.

James Otieno was one of ten people to take part in the first pilot of the Silicon Valley Encore Fellows program.

THEN; NOW

Holly Thibodeaux
Ontario, California

I'm the oldest of seven children, and neither of my parents went to college. When I was fifteen, I started working as a maid. I tell people that I was an assistant maid to the assistant maid at a retirement hotel. College wasn't even on my radar screen until I was a senior in high school. I devoured books, but I was really one of those iffy students. I didn't have any discipline, but when I found something I was wild about, I excelled.

The last year of high school I really turned on. I wanted to go to college. I was able to get in on probationary status at LaVerne College, seventy miles away from home. I went one semester, then met a guy, got mononucleosis, and dropped out. We ended up getting married the next August, and we were married for ten years.

I've never had a career, just a string of medical-clerical jobs that I hated. I was a single mom raising two children, but whenever time and money would allow, I took college classes. I loved learning and was good at it. There was a feeling of satisfaction and pride in my educational successes that I never found in my employment. I dreamed of being a college professor, of a life of scholarship and bright conversations, of the status and how proud my children and family would be, of being able to make enough money to pay the bills. For thirty years, I kept my eye on the prize of a college degree that, like some mirage on a hot highway, seemed to recede the older I got.

I've always been pretty fearful. I was afraid of humiliating myself. But that started to change around age fifty. I honestly think it had to do with losing my looks. I never looked like a model or anything, but from a very young age, I attracted attention, but I didn't know what to do with that. What I knew was that it was some kind of power, but I was really afraid of it. As I got older and that was fading, I felt less afraid somehow.

At that time, in my fifties, I felt more confident and secure in myself, but I also had real economic fear. I had nothing, zero, zilch. I had always been able to find a job that was okay. I could make enough. And then, all of sudden, in my late fifties, with the economy tanking, I lost two jobs, and I thought, "Oh, my God, I'm not going to be able to get another one." I accumulated a lot of debt, and I got to a point where I thought, "This is crazy." My family offered to help, but I knew that if I let them bail me out, it would crush my soul. It was better to go through bankruptcy and move on than to accept help and feel like I was totally dependent on them.

Soon afterward, I got a call from my son, who had graduated college and started a business and was doing well. He asked if I would like a car. I hadn't been able to afford a car for years. I just laughed and told him I didn't need a car, I was fine, and I gave him a lecture on putting some money in a retirement fund. He told me I did need a car, so I could get to the local college and finish my degree. That was the deal: He would get me a car if I promised to finish now. I said okay and went back to the community college. Going back to school cost me my last job, and I let that happen. I just thought, "Oh, well, here we go."

The rest, as they say, is history. I graduated magna cum laude from California Baptist University in May 2008. I had done it! I always thought that everything would fall into place if I could just finish. But then I had education loans to pay back, no job, and no confidence that I could translate my scholastic success into employment.

My son is a very focused man, and he had a great deal more faith in me than I had in myself. He told me, "Don't lose your momentum!" and pushed me to look for graduate programs. I had no idea what I was doing. I knew I wanted to study ancient philosophy, so I just put it in Google, and one of the first schools that came up was Claremont. And then they let me in! Most people's reaction when I say that I'm going to study ancient philosophy is, "*Whhhaaattt* are you going to do with that?" But I wanted to know the examined life. Why am I here? Why are *we* here? The big questions just light my fire. My heart rate goes up. I also think you have to be pretty smart to learn this stuff, so if I'm smart enough to learn it, I could probably teach it. And that's a better job than I've ever had.

I sure wish that I knew a whole lot more about getting financing. But I got student loans, and my son and daughter are filling in the rest. When

I start panicking about the amount of debt I'm adding, I think, "Okay, I'll just be paying it off for the rest of my days."

I feel like there's so much I don't know and that I've just got to keep moving. Last year I was kind of just stumbling around in a fog. Now I really have to push. And this year I really have to formulate in my mind what I'm going to do to make a living. I want that to fit with my passions. If I can get a grasp on what's possible, I think I'm creative enough to find a niche. And that's making me really hopeful. For once in my life, I'm going to love going to work. I don't know how I'm going to do that, but I will.

Holly Thibodeaux received her Masters of Arts in Philosophy from Claremont Graduate University in May 2011.

THEN; NOW

Ted Butchart
Charlottesville, Virginia

I reached a point, when I was forty-nine, when I was no longer happy doing the work in natural building design and in teaching that I'd been doing. Something was shifting in me, which happens about every seven years. It used to be an odd feeling. It's like, "Why am I no longer satisfied doing what I loved doing yesterday?" Now I actually recognize the feeling and just kind of look around expectantly, like, "Okay, what's next? Something even better is coming along."

At forty-nine I was right in the middle of one of these changes. I talked to my wife, Ellen, and we agreed that I could have six months to be lost. She agreed that we could afford for me to work less and less doing design while I figured this out, which is a huge gift. I mean, you can't put money on that, to allow someone to just be lost and not be bringing money in and not know what they're doing. That was a huge gift, because these shifts don't happen overnight.

I didn't know what I wanted to do next. At any point, for almost the entire six months, you could have walked up to me on the street and said, "What is it that you really want to do?" and I could not have told you. I asked myself: Do I want to write more? Do I want to do design work, but with other people, instead of just by myself? Do I need to shift into a different kind of design, not be quite so focused on the natural materials? What is it? Nothing was really jelling for me. My income stream was definitely dwindling, and I was actually approaching the end of the six months. It was like, "Okay, I've got to find something to do."

We went to dinner one night with a workmate of Ellen's, and his wife was at Bastyr University in Seattle, training to be a naturopathic physician, with a specialty in homeopathy. Even as I talked to her, nothing was clicking. And the next morning, I woke up and I thought, "I know exactly what I want to do—become a naturopathic doctor." When I realized that, it was like, "Why did it take so long to figure this out?" Because this is what I've always wanted to do, all the way from undergraduate years, back when I realized that there was no way I could afford med school. And, truly, a day before, if you'd asked me, "What is your deepest heart's desire?" this would not have come up.

The morning after I had this epiphany, I realized that they cut off applications about ten days later. So I zipped around and got all my transcripts to them. I was the oldest person in my class. At fifty it was harder for me to memorize huge, long lists, maybe, than it was for a twenty-five-year-old, but I knew where to put the information because I had a framework already. So they're just taking notes, writing it down, trying to memorize all of it, and I'm sitting there going, "Oh, my God, this answers that question, or this information goes right here." So in a lot of ways, it was actually easier for me as an older student than it was for the young ones.

The program, which I did full time for nearly four years, was the hardest thing I've ever done in my life. I just don't know that some of my younger classmates have the life experience to really sit with somebody and be able to determine, "This is depression. Nope, this is actually grief, and grief needs to be lived, not medicated," and to talk to people about that. When people come in with what's obviously a terminal disease, I don't take it as my only mission to try to save their life. I try to guide them a bit through a good death, if that's what's in front of them. I just don't think that a twenty-five- or thirty-year-old is really, I mean, with few exceptions, how are they going to do that? You have to have tasted a little of your own mortality to calmly sit and talk to somebody about theirs.

It's been about ten years since my last seven-year itch. It's difficult because I'm a very restless sort. I was born on the Oregon coast, looking out over the ocean, thinking, "What's over there?" But I've found something I love to do that's useful to other people and intriguing enough to me so that I want to keep learning.

Somebody asked me, "Well, when are you going to retire?" I looked at them kind of cross-eyed. I just took on a $100,000 student loan. I will work until I die, and when I die, the student loan is forgiven. That's my retirement plan.

Ted Butchart has worked as a general contractor, a software designer, an architect, a natural building construction designer, and a teacher. He is now a naturopathic doctor.

THEN; NOW

Ellen Butchart
Charlottesville, Virginia

I went on an extraordinary trip to India in 2008 with my sister. Like many people who travel to India, I was extremely moved by what I saw there. There was a sense of humanity up close. I started to notice how people lived together and felt how hard life was for all the people I was meeting or seeing. It was a struggle to be a human being in that environment, and it just transformed my senses. I was all of a sudden feeling really close to the world.

When I came back, I felt like I had to be more concerned with what I was doing. I wanted to do something that somehow helped the world, really changed the way people lived, something to make their burden a little lighter.

And then I came home and lost my job. I started from ground zero at that point. I hadn't ever thought, "Well, what do you want to do with your life?" Instead, it was always, "Oh, okay, here's the next job." I hadn't actually ever been unemployed for more than six weeks since I was about seventeen years old, so this was a really interesting experience . . . and a pretty painful one.

I never once thought of not working. I love working. I love being on a team, having a project. I wanted to put myself in a position to be a candidate for a job, and I realized I needed to have more tools.

At the same time, my husband—we were both in our fifties at the time—had just finished medical school. He really believed that he could bring his experience and ability to the big picture about medicine and about people. It was an incredibly successful experience for him, and he kept exponentially growing as a doctor. I watched him learning, and it was an inspiration for me to think about going back to school, too.

So I started looking at MBA programs that were nontraditional in their approach to both teaching and curriculum. I talked to a friend who was at the Bainbridge Graduate Institute (BGI) in Seattle, which offers an MBA in sustainable business, and I decided this was the place I needed to be. It had all the things I was looking for: community and a real emphasis on business as leadership and on transformative change.

I was as excited about business school as I was when I started in the technology field twenty years ago. I felt like, "Here I am again, able to help build a vision and not be passive and learn, but be part of things, creating and learning at the same time."

BGI is a phenomenal community. Ninety percent of the students are twenty or more years younger than I am, and it's just great to know that they are trying to learn about the difficult things in the world, thinking about social justice, thinking about the environment, thinking about the things that are at risk, at such risk, and also learning accounting. And they are really present for one another with a kind of emotional honesty that is very, very profound. I can't believe there's a school that would foster that kind of relationship building. I joke about it—it's like Hogwarts! We go out for a weekend once a month, and we're in this magical place, Island Wood, and sometimes we spontaneously sing at dinner.

There's a lot of intentional community at work, and from my own experience in business, that intentional community is going to accelerate innovation and creativity and bring confidence to people. When people break out of the constructs of the bottom line and profit, the real growth comes from being expansive in your vision.

I feel immensely grateful that I went from being cynical and pretty beaten up in my life in business to this, to going to this place of power. And I've regained my voice.

A lot of friends ask me why I bother going back to school, and it's hard to express all of what I've experienced. And it really won't be powerful or palatable until I do something and I say, "Here, this is why I did it." At this point, I'm not really sure where I'm going to end up, but a lot of ideas are lighting up in my brain.

A recent conversation with my oldest son put things in perspective for me. After he got his undergraduate degree, he worked for a number of years, and he kept trying to figure out what he wanted to do next. And then, just after he got into law school, we had this really interesting conversation. He said, "You know, Mom, I decided to do it your way."

And I said, "What do you mean, 'my way'? I have a way?"

And he said, "Yes, I stopped trying to figure out what I wanted to do at the end of it all. I just started. I started down the path to the journey, and I'm not worried about what I will do at the end."

I always thought of "my way" as jumping off a cliff and bouncing down the mountain all the way. But over the years, I survived and I flourished. It took a long time and it wasn't easy, but I didn't end up in a worse place. Having that knowledge helps.

At the beginning, there aren't many people who are incredibly courageous. It's only *after* you learn that you survive that it makes it easier to try.

Ellen Butchart has worked as a university teacher, a producer of educational CD-ROMs, senior design manager at Amazon.com, and director of content development of Rosetta Stone.

THEN; NOW

Anne Nolan
Providence, Rhode Island

When I went to work for the corporate world many, many years ago, it was exciting, and it was new, and I was doing things I'd never done and learning things. And it was incredibly exciting. But over the years I lost a sense of purpose. I wasn't quite sure why I was doing it. I mean, I knew why I was working. I was working for the money. I simply became more and more emotionally distant, and it was less fulfilling. Still, the president of the company was a wonderful man, and we did good work—we cleaned up the environment. But I didn't clean up the environment. I was in corporate.

Then, one day in 1999, we made the decision to dissolve the company. It was the right business decision to make, definitely. It's not easy to say this, but I guess I wasn't invested enough to really feel any grief about its being over. I did receive a year's salary as severance, which gave me the opportunity to say, "Okay, what's next?"

That year of reflection was an important part of my journey. Three months into the year, it just kind of hit me that I couldn't do another corporate job. I don't think I was really ever cut out for the corporate world. I mean, I'm a product of the sixties, for crying out loud. I need to feel passionate about my work. I need to do something that makes me cry, for good reasons, and I hadn't felt that kind of commitment or passion about a job in years and years.

I was never a walker before that year, but I started walking every day, six or seven miles along the Blackstone River and canal. It was a form of meditation for me. I often had what-if-I-win-the-lottery thoughts, which I've had for twenty or thirty years now, ever since I've been buying tickets. I always have the same fantasy, that if I won the lottery, I would start a not-for-profit dealing with homeless families. I also want a house on the ocean, but it was just one of those what-if-I-win-the-lottery things. I can't afford a house on the ocean, and I thought I couldn't afford to run a homeless program.

One day, I realized that I was being really stupid, that I had been working for money for so long, and it was time that I worked for passion, and I just had to make the money work. Was I going to spend the rest of my life making money and being unhappy or not making money and being happy? That's what it got down to. I was just so sure about my decision. I knew what I wanted and wouldn't listen to anyone who discouraged me. It was like, "Get out of my way, honey, because somehow I'm going to do this."

A number of people told me that I should go to a little place called Travelers Aid in downtown Providence. I had never heard of it, and in my mind it was something in a bus terminal. But eventually I called the woman who was president and asked if I could have a tour. On the day of my appointment, I turned into the building, and I opened the door and—true story—I started to cry. I was overwhelmed by the humanity of the place and the people and the pain.

It was just this awful building with a dirty stairway going down into a basement. And at the bottom of the stairs there was a desk, and the place was packed with people. I mean *packed*, men and women and some very sick people and some crazy, inebriated people, and people who were terrified and people who were just terrifying. And I was terrified on top of it all. I couldn't talk, I was so overwhelmed by what I saw.

I met the woman who was president, and she took me on a tour. She asked me to join the board that day and then said, "But I need to tell you that at the end of the year, I'm leaving." And it was like, "Yes, okay, here's your hat, what's your hurry?" I just knew it was the job I wanted.

I joined the board, and five months later, when the president's position became open, I applied. I almost didn't get it. Another candidate had a lot of experience in the not-for-profit world, and the story I'm told is that the committee voted for her, but the chairman of the board at the time changed his vote. The rest is history. It's been nearly ten years now, and it's the best thing I've ever done in my life. We changed the name from Travelers Aid to Crossroads. We do a lot of housing now and we're statewide, and we deal with all kinds of issues that we weren't dealing with before. I want to continue to grow the organization, do more housing, do more job training. I have no plans to leave for a while, that's for sure. I love my world here very much, and I love this organization. I have learned so much. And mostly what I've learned is to appreciate my life so much more.

I'm making all this sound like it's wonderful and grand, but the one part that hasn't been easy is the financial part. It's been very hard to adjust to making half of what I was making. I thought I would simply do less and learn to economize and cut back and blah, blah, blah. The first year I managed okay, but I went through a lot of savings. And then I started living off the equity in my house, which, given the housing market, is pretty much gone now. Let me just say that I'm still trying to figure this out.

At the same time, I wouldn't change my position for anything. It's just so enriching. There's no way I could ever go back to the corporate world—ever, ever, ever.

Anne Nolan has been president of Crossroads, the largest homeless service organization in Rhode Island, since 2001.

THEN; NOW

Mark Noonan
Portland, Oregon

My wife died in 2004, and all the grieving and mourning sent me spinning, about what was the purpose of life. I did a lot of reflecting on how I was spending my time.

I had had a great career in high-tech, starting in 1977. I was at Intel. I was at IBM. I was at several smaller start-up companies. It was a really great experience, very rewarding, both financially and careerwise.

And then the new century rolled in, and as the world economy changed, my job got a lot tougher. The early days in Silicon Valley, when you could pick any parking lot and drive in and get a job, were long gone. I was spending a lot of time downsizing and outsourcing engineering work, sending manufacturing offshore. And I felt like my work was more about tearing down communities and breaking up families. That didn't feel right, since my real reason for working was centered around family and keeping that going.

For two years after my wife died, I tried to reenergize my feelings about the high-tech world. Then, at a certain point, I just realized that I didn't have the heart for it anymore. I wanted to do something where I was giving back a little more. Some of the idealism I'd had in the sixties was still there. I wanted to do work that would feed my soul and not just my pocketbook.

So I went to management and said I'd just rather package out at this point. At the time, if you could show that your job was going away because of outsourcing, there was federal money for retraining. I was able to sit down and think about what kind of work would really excite me for the next fifteen or twenty years. I'm a ruminator, so I took two or three months just to consider options. I had an opportunity to go to a career counselor, as part of my buyout package. I actually decided not to do that, even though it was a benefit. I just had pretty good confidence that I could work through it on my own. And that's pretty much what I did.

I considered going to chef school, taking a class on a cruise ship. I did some market research. I tried to follow my heart. I had friends point me in different directions. And I started exploring the gerontology world and social services around aging.

I didn't have the privilege of having a lot of grandparents when I was growing up, so I can't say that I was drawn to the field from a pure stance of wanting to help older people. It was more from pure potential and need and what I thought would be some real job opportunities. By the year 2020, about a third of the population will be fifty-five and older. People are living much longer, and they're going to live a lot healthier, and they're going to want to do things. That just said to me that this is a growing market. And I started getting excited in a way that I haven't since the high-tech bubble was just starting up.

I was fifty-two at the time, and the last thing I wanted to do was study for three or four years for an entirely new career. So I was looking pretty closely at the community colleges around here for a one- to two-year program that could get me back out to the job market rapidly. I have a BS in engineering, so I didn't have to worry about any general requirements. I was able to get an associate's degree in gerontology in a year and a half.

It was very intimidating to think about going back to school—the idea of being on campus and roaming around with the coeds and being the only white-haired person in the class. But at Portland Community College, I was able to do my entire course of study online. I had great discussions online with people I never met.

I had years of management experience, and I kind of locked into the idea that I loved helping volunteers find their niche, find what they wanted to do. I did three internships—one with our local Meals on Wheels in a senior center, one with our local AARP, and one with the Northwest Oregon Volunteer Association. In each case, I worked with the volunteer manager and got a résumé item and made contacts. I did a fourth internship with Elders in Action, and out of that I learned some valuable skills, and I got to be known, and I got to know them. And when a job came open there, I was in the right place at the right time.

I started as a program specialist, working to help refer people to resources they needed or mediate disputes. And then I moved into a job matching needs with volunteers. And now, given all my previous high-tech experience, I've been able to create a new job with the ostentatious title of social media manager. I work with Facebook and Twitter to reach out to our partners and to potential donors and to get the word out. It's actually been a lot of fun. You have to become a fan on our Facebook page!

When I think about the big picture, I wasn't lucky in the sense that my encore career really came out of tragedy. But I feel fortunate now to have been able to find work that I love and to know that I want to keep doing it, and growing with it, for a long, long time.

Mark Noonan has been working at Elders in Action for the past four years.

NOTES

CHAPTER 1: AN AARP DISCOUNT—AND TWO CRIBS

2 *The lightness reminded me of research:* Jennifer L. Aaker, Melanie Rudd, and Cassie Mogilner, "If Money Doesn't Make You Happy, Consider Time," *Journal of Consumer Psychology* 21, no. 2 (2011): 126–130.

5 *New research suggests that children:* Kaare Christensen et al., "Ageing Populations: The Challenges Ahead," *Lancet* 374, no. 9696 (2009): 1196–1208.

9 *A few months earlier, I'd picked up the Sunday:* Jenny Hourihan Bailin, "Out of a Job, and Realizing Change Is Good," *New York Times*, October 25, 2008, http://www.nytimes.com/2008/10/26/jobs/26pre.html.

11 *"living longer and thinking shorter":* Mary Catherine Bateson, *Composing a Further Life: The Age of Active Wisdom* (New York: Alfred A. Knopf, 2010).

12 *"unstable social space":* Thomas R. Cole, "The Prophecy of Senescence: G. Stanley Hall and the Reconstruction of Old Age in America," *Gerontologist* 24, no. 4 (1984): 360–366.

12 *a bookkeeper named Ida May Fuller:* W. Andrew Achenbaum, "What Is Retirement For?" *Wilson Quarterly* (Spring 2006).

12 *"too old to work, too young to die":* Nelson Lichtenstein, *The Most Dangerous Man in Detroit: Walter Reuther and the Fate of American Labor* (New York: Basic Books, 1995).

13 *with something called the "golden years":* Marc Freedman, *Encore: Finding Work That Matters in the Second Half of Life* (New York: PublicAffairs, 2007).

13 *in his book* Reset: Kurt Andersen, *Reset: How This Crisis Can Restore Our Values and Renew America* (New York: Random House, 2009).

15 *In Nora Ephron's words:* Deborah Solomon, "Questions for Nora Ephron," *New York Times Magazine*, May 6, 2007, http://query.nytimes.com/gst/fullpage.html?res=9401E6D9133EF935A35756 C0A9619C8B63.

15 *Daphne Merkin describes:* Daphne Merkin, "Reinventing Middle Age," *New York Times Magazine*, May 6, 2007, http://www.nytimes.com/2007/05/06/magazine/06WWLN-Lede-t.html.

CHAPTER 2: ONE RIVER AT A TIME

19 *Joseph Campbell said midlife:* Joseph Campbell, *The Hero's Journey: Joseph Campbell on His Life and Work* (New York: Harper and Row, 1990).

21 *Harvard sociologist Sara Lawrence-Lightfoot:* Sara Lawrence-Lightfoot, *The Third Chapter: Passion, Risk, and Adventure in the 25 Years After 50* (New York: Farrar, Straus, and Giroux, 2009).

22, 24 *"We like to live large" and "I actually one night sat down":* Meredith McKenzie, interview by Sam Eaton, "Putting a New Value on the Golden Years," *Marketplace*, NPR, May 15, 2009, http://marketplace.publicradio.org/display/web/2009/05/15/nad_pm_eaton_retirement.

25 *McKenzie has also come to embody:* Chris Farrell, *The New Frugality: How to Consume Less, Save More, and Live Better* (New York: Bloomsbury Press, 2009).

CHAPTER 3: A WORLD OUT OF WHACK

30 *the concept was invented by a Canadian:* Elliott Jaques, "Death and the Midlife Crisis," *International Journal of Psychoanalysis* 46 (1965): 502–514.

31 *Critic Jeff Roush:* Susan Krauss Whitbourne, "That Certain Age: Does It Have to Mean Crisis?" *Psychology Today* (blog), December 8, 2009, http://www.psychologytoday.com/blog/fulfillment-any-age/200912/certain-age-does-it-have-mean-crisis.

31   *Ray Romano has commented:* Margy Rochlin, "Taking on Midlife and All Its Crises," *New York Times*, November 29, 2009.

31   *Shellenbarger describes her own descent:* Sue Shellenbarger, *The Breaking Point: How Today's Women Are Navigating the Midlife Crisis* (New York: Henry Holt, 2005).

32   *It was followed by a* Time *cover story:* Nancy Gibbs, "A Female Midlife Crisis? Bring It On!" *Time*, May 8, 2005, http://www.time .com/time/magazine/article/0,9171,1059032,00.html.

32   *Bronwyn Fryer, a former editor at the* Harvard Business Review: Bronwyn Fryer, "Coping with 'Career Menopause,'" *Harvard Business Review* (blog), October 28, 2009, http://blogs.hbr.org/hbr/ hbreditors/2009/10/coping_with_career_menopause.html.

32   *A major MacArthur Foundation research initiative:* Winifred Gallagher, "Midlife Myths," *Atlantic Monthly*, May 1993, http://www .theatlantic.com/past/docs/issues/93may/gallagher.htm. See also Orville Gilbert Brim et al., eds., *How Healthy Are We? A National Study of Well-Being at Midlife* (Chicago: University of Chicago Press, 2004); and Margie E. Lachman and Jacquelyn Boone James, eds., *Multiple Paths of Midlife Development* (Chicago: University of Chicago Press, 1997).

36   *One common new-stage oxymoron:* Mark Penn, *Microtrends: The Small Forces Behind Tomorrow's Big Changes* (New York: Hachette Book Group, 2007).

38   *Writing in the British medical journal* The Lancet: Kaare Christensen et al., "Ageing Populations: The Challenges Ahead," *Lancet* 374, no. 9696 (2009): 1196–1208.

39   *Jack Rosenthal, the Pulitzer Prize–winning former editor:* Jack Rosenthal, "Wellderly," *New York Times Magazine*, July 22, 2007, http://www.nytimes.com/2007/07/22/magazine/22wwln-guest-t .html.

40   Time *offers this headline:* Lisa Takeuchi Cullen, "How Not to Look Old on the Job: More Boomers Are Working into Their Senior Years, and Who Wants to Look Like the Office Geezer?" *Time*, February 29, 2008, http://www.time.com/time/magazine/article/0,9171, 1718568,00.html.

41   *The writer, Christopher Noxon:* Christopher Noxon, *Rejuvenile: Kickball, Cartoons, Cupcakes, and the Reinvention of the American Grown-Up* (New York: Three Rivers Press, 2006).

42 *two* New York Times *columns:* Nicholas D. Kristof, "Geezers Doing Good," *New York Times*, July 20, 2008, http://www.nytimes.com/2008/07/20/opinion/20kristof.html; David Brooks, "The Geezers' Crusade," *New York Times*, February 1, 2010, http://www.nytimes.com/2010/02/02/opinion/02brooks.html.

43 *The late Daniel Boorstin:* Betty Friedan, *The Fountain of Age* (New York: Touchstone, 1993).

47 *pick up a copy of the January–February 2010 issue:* Jack A. Goldstone, "The New Population Bomb: The Four Megatrends That Will Change the World," *Foreign Affairs*, January–February 2010.

48 *Economist Laurence Kotlikoff, in his book:* Laurence J. Kotlikoff and Scott Burns, *The Coming Generational Storm: What You Need to Know About America's Economic Future* (Cambridge: MIT Press, 2004).

49 *Shoven poses a simple question:* John B. Shoven, "New Age Thinking," *Foreign Policy*, December 13, 2007.

51 *In his satirical novel:* Christopher Buckley, *Boomsday* (New York: Twelve, 2007).

51 *others wonder out loud:* Charles Mann, "The Coming Death Shortage," *Atlantic Monthly*, May 2005; Gregory Rodriguez, "Can We Be Too Healthy and Live Too Long?" *Los Angeles Times*, April 19, 2010.

52 *what author Matt Miller calls the tyranny:* Matt Miller, *The Tyranny of Dead Ideas: Letting Go of the Old Ways of Thinking to Unleash a New Prosperity* (New York: Times Books, 2009).

CHAPTER 4: NEW-STAGE THINKING

57 *discovering findings and recommendations:* The Carnegie Inquiry into the Third Age, *Final Report: Life, Work, and Livelihood in the Third Age* (Dunfermline: Carnegie United Kingdom Trust, 1992).

58 *Peter Laslett's book that launched the ship:* Peter Laslett, *A Fresh Map of Life: The Emergence of the Third Age* (Cambridge: Harvard University Press, 1991).

58 Material by and about Peter Laslett derives from many sources, including: Eric Midwinter, *500 Beacons: The U3A Story* (London: Third Age Press, 2004); John Dunn and Tony Wrigley, "Thomas Peter Ruffell Laslett: 1915–2001," *Proceedings of the British Acad-*

emy (London: British Academy, 2006); Quentin Skinner and Tony Wrigley, "Peter Laslett," *Guardian*, November 17, 2001; "Peter Laslett," *Independent*, November 24, 2001; Asa Briggs, *Michael Young: Social Entrepreneur* (Basingstoke, UK: Palgrave Macmillan, 2001); and various articles by Laslett, including "The Emergence of the Third Age," *Ageing and Society* 7, no. 2 (1987): 133–160.

66 *Some scholars suggest that Shakespeare's seven ages:* All these divisions come from Ben Schott, "On the Division of Our Three Score & Ten," *New York Times*, October 19, 2009.

67 *"Stages of life are artifacts":* Jill Lepore, "Baby Talk: The Fuss About Parenthood," *New Yorker*, June 29, 2009.

67 *Writing in* Daedalus *in the 1970s:* Tamara K. Hareven, "The Last Stage: Historical Adulthood and Old Age," *Daedalus* 105, no. 4 (1976): 13–27.

69 Information and quotes from G. Stanley Hall come from these sources, among others: G. Stanley Hall, *Senescence: The Last Half of Life* (New York: D. Appleton, 1922); Thomas Hine, *The Rise and Fall of the American Teenager* (New York: Harper Perennial, 2000); Grace Palladino, *Teenagers: An American History* (New York: Basic Books, 1996); Jon Savage, *Teenage: The Prehistory of Youth Culture, 1875–1945* (New York: Penguin, 2008); Kathleen Woodward, "Against Wisdom: The Social Politics of Anger and Aging," *Journal of Aging Studies* 17 (2003): 55–67; Manon Parry, "G. Stanley Hall: Psychologist and Early Gerontologist," *American Journal of Public Health* 96, no. 7 (2006): 1160–1162; Thomas R. Cole, "The Prophecy of Senescence: G. Stanley Hall and the Reconstruction of Old Age in America," *Gerontologist* 24, no. 4 (1984): 360–366; and Dorothy Ross, "Granville Stanley Hall," in vol. 9 of *American National Biography* (New York: Oxford University Press, 1999) and *G. Stanley Hall: The Psychologist as Prophet* (Chicago: University of Chicago Press, 1972).

77 *New-Stage Sequels:* Betty Friedan, *The Feminine Mystique* (New York: W. W. Norton, 1963) and *The Fountain of Age* (New York: Touchstone, 1993); Gloria Steinem, *Doing Sixty & Seventy* (San Francisco: Elders Academy Press, 2006); Suzanne Braun Levine, *Fifty Is the New Fifty: Ten Life Lessons for Women in Second Adulthood* (New York: Viking Penguin, 2009) and *Inventing the Rest of Our Lives: Women in Second Adulthood* (New York: Viking Penguin,

2005); Sara Lawrence-Lightfoot, *The Third Chapter: Passion, Risk, and Adventure in the 25 Years After 50* (New York: Farrar, Straus, and Giroux, 2009); Mary Catherine Bateson, *Composing a Further Life: The Age of Active Wisdom* (New York: Alfred A. Knopf, 2010), *Willing to Learn: Passages of Personal Discovery* (Hanover, NH: Steer Forth Press, 2004), and "The HBR List: Breakthrough Ideas for 2005," *Harvard Business Review*, February 2005.

82 *In addition to the Third Age:* Phyllis Moen and Patricia Roehling, *The Career Mystique: Cracks in the American Dream* (Lanham, MD: Rowman and Littlefield, 2004); Ken Dychtwald, *Age Power: How the 21st Century Will Be Ruled by the New Old* (New York: Penguin Putnam, 1999); Laura L. Carstensen, *A Long Bright Future: An Action Plan for a Lifetime of Happiness, Health, and Financial Security* (New York: Broadway Books, 2009); Carlo Strenger and Arie Ruttenberg, "The Existential Necessity of Midlife Change," *Harvard Business Review*, February 2008; "Interview with Carlo Strenger," *Learning to Lead Interview*, February 2009; Charles Handy, *The Hungry Spirit* (New York: Broadway Books, 1998) and *The Age of Unreason* (Boston: Harvard Business School Press, 1989).

CHAPTER 5: THE NEXT MAP OF LIFE

90 *It's a point made by:* Barbara Strauch, *The Secret Life of the Grown-Up Brain: The Surprising Talents of the Middle-Aged Mind* (New York: Viking, 2010).

90 *a recent University of Michigan study:* Igor Grossmanna et al., "Reasoning About Social Conflicts Improves into Old Age," *Proceedings of the National Academy of Sciences of the United States of America* 107, no. 16 (2010).

90 *Eleanor Roosevelt got this point:* Eleanor Roosevelt, *You Learn by Living: Eleven Keys for a More Fulfilling Life* (Philadelphia: Westminster Press, 1960).

91 *a simultaneous compression and expansion of time:* Sarah Kershaw, "A Troubling Timeline for a Certain Age Group," *New York Times*, September 17, 2009, http://query.nytimes.com/gst/fullpage.html?res=9403E3DC143BF934A2575AC0A96F9C8B63.

92 *Stephen Hall calls this shift:* Stephen S. Hall, *Wisdom: From Philosophy to Neuroscience* (New York: Alfred A. Knopf, 2010).

92 Quotes from Laura Carstensen come from the following: Laura L. Carstensen, *A Long Bright Future: An Action Plan for a Lifetime of Happiness, Health, and Financial Security* (New York: Broadway Books, 2009); Stephen S. Hall, *Wisdom: From Philosophy to Neuroscience* (New York: Alfred A. Knopf, 2010); Barbara Strauch, *The Secret Life of the Grown-Up Brain: The Surprising Talents of the Middle-Aged Mind* (New York: Viking, 2010); and Jonathan Weiner, *Long for This World: The Strange Science of Immortality* (New York: HarperCollins, 2010).

93 *in the commencement address Apple founder Steve Jobs gave:* http://www.youtube.com/watch?v=UF8uR6Z6KLc.

94 *management expert Daniel Pink adds:* Daniel H. Pink, *Drive: The Surprising Truth About What Motivates Us* (New York: Riverhead Books, 2009).

95 *Time Beyond:* Erik H. Erikson, Joan M. Erikson, and Helen Q. Kivnick, *Vital Involvement in Old Age* (New York: W. W. Norton, 1994); Erik H. Erikson, *Identity: Youth and Crisis* (New York: W. W. Norton, 1968); John Kotre, *Outliving the Self: Generativity and the Interpretation of Lives* (Baltimore: Johns Hopkins University Press, 1984); Ed De St. Aubin, Dan P. McAdams, and Tae-Chang Kim, eds., *The Generative Society: Caring for Future Generations* (Washington, DC: American Psychological Association, 2003); Dan P. McAdams, *The Redemptive Self: Stories Americans Live By* (Oxford: Oxford University Press, 2005); George E. Vaillant, *Adaptation to Life* (Boston: Little, Brown, 1977) and *Aging Well: Surprising Guideposts to a Happier Life from the Landmark Harvard Study of Adult Development* (Boston: Little, Brown, 2002); John Snarey, *How Fathers Care for the Next Generation: A Four-Decade Study* (Cambridge: Harvard University Press, 1993).

95 *The late American historian Christopher Lasch:* Christopher Lasch, "Aging in a Culture Without a Future," *Hastings Center Report* (August 1977).

97 *conducted a longitudinal study:* Susan Krauss Whitbourne, *The Search for Fulfillment: Revolutionary New Research That Reveals the Secret to Long-Term Happiness* (New York: Ballantine Books, 2010).

CHAPTER 6: ROUTES OF PASSAGE

105 Paula Lopez Crespin's story and her quotes are culled from several interviews with her, including time at the Cole Arts and Science Academy in Denver, as well as this portrait of her: Cecilia Capuzzi Simon, "So You Want to Be a Teacher for America?" *New York Times*, July 26, 2009, http://www.nytimes.com/2009/07/26/education/edlife/26continuinged-t.html. Two quotes come directly from this article: "I was sitting in the back and wanted to wave to her, but she was in a zone, in command" and "She was the best teacher I had ever seen."

112 *insights fit the perspective of:* William Bridges, *Transitions: Making Sense of Life's Changes* (New York: Perseus Books, 1980). Also informing this section is an unpublished paper: Beth Benjamin, "GSB Encore Initiative: A Campaign to Improve Senior Leadership Transitions Through Shared Learning and Community."

121 *the Sacred Heart School of Theology:* Jonathan Englert, *The Collar* (New York: Houghton Mifflin, 2006).

121 *The program is the brainchild of three leading lights:* Rosabeth Moss Kanter, Rakesh Khurana, and Nitin Nohria, "Moving Higher Education to Its Next Stage: A New Set of Societal Challenges, a New Stage of Life, and a Call to Action for Universities" (working paper, Harvard Business School, 2005).

124 *the Silicon Valley Encore Fellows program:* Sarah Kershaw, "Ready for Life's Encore Performances," *New York Times*, March 19, 2010, http://www.nytimes.com/2010/03/21/fashion/21age.html. See also Kelly Greene, "Law Opens Up 'Encore' Careers," *Wall Street Journal*, April 2, 2009, http://online.wsj.com/article/SB123863704304281321.html.

125 *"We like to think that the key":* Herminia Ibarra, *Working Identity: Unconventional Strategies for Reinventing Your Career* (Boston: Harvard Business School Press, 2003).

125 *According to a CareerBuilder survey:* CareerBuilder, "Experienced, Mature Workers to Compete with College Students for Internships This Fall, Finds New CareerBuilder Survey," August 11, 2010, http://www.careerbuilder.com/share/aboutus/pressreleasesdetail.aspx?id=pr582&sd=8/11/2010&ed=08/11/2010.

127 *The School of Life is located in a storefront:* http://www.theschooloflife.com.

CHAPTER 7: TEN STEPS TOWARD A NEW STAGE

131 *Carl Jung argued that:* Carl Jung, "The Stages of Life," in *The Structure and Dynamics of the Psyche,* by Carl Jung (Princeton: Princeton University Press, 1969).

131 *In her groundbreaking "Grandmother Hypothesis":* Kristen Hawkes, "Grandmothers and the Evolution of Human Longevity," *American Journal of Human Biology* 15 (2003).

132 *Historian Jill Lepore:* Jill Lepore, "Baby Talk: The Fuss About Parenthood," *New Yorker,* June 29, 2009.

135 *the "optimal design for a new stage of life":* Laura L. Carstensen, "On the Brink of a Brand-New Old Age," *New York Times,* January 2, 2001.

135 *it's almost as if the GPS program:* I'm indebted to my former colleague John Gomperts for this image.

139 *A 2010 study from the RAND Corporation:* Nicole Maestas, "Back to Work: Expectations and Realizations of Work After Retirement," *Journal of Human Resources* 45, no. 3 (2010): 718–748.

139 *In Britain, for example, there are an estimated 200,000:* Geraldine Bedell and Rowena Young, eds., *The New Old Age: Perspectives on Innovating Our Way to the Good Life for All* (London: National Endowment for Science, Technology, and the Arts, 2009), http://www.nesta.org.uk/library/documents/the-new-old-age.pdf.

139 *Daniel Pink suggests:* Daniel H. Pink, *Drive: The Surprising Truth About What Motivates Us* (New York: Riverhead Books, 2009).

142 *As Harvard's Rosabeth Moss Kanter has argued:* Rosabeth Moss Kanter, Rakesh Khurana, and Nitin Nohria, "Moving Higher Education to Its Next Stage: A New Set of Societal Challenges, a New Stage of Life, and a Call to Action for Universities" (working paper, Harvard Business School, 2005).

146 *In their article in* Harvard Business Review: Carlo Strenger and Arie Ruttenberg, "The Existential Necessity of Midlife Change," *Harvard Business Review,* February 2008.

147 *Individual Purpose Accounts:* Tara Siegel Bernard, "How to Bear the Tuition Burden Without a Paycheck," *New York Times,* August 20, 2009, http://www.nytimes.com/2009/08/20/education/20COST.html.

151 *the most significant step of all:* U.S. Congress, Senate, Committee on Finance, *Choosing to Work During Retirement and the Impact on*

Social Security: Hearing Before the Committee on Finance, testimony of Marc Freedman, founder and chief executive officer of Civic Ventures, 111th Cong., 2nd sess., July 15, 2010, http://finance.senate .gov/imo/media/doc/071510mftest.pdf.

153   *It's time to bring together:* For more ideas on a comprehensive and coherent policy agenda for the new stage, see Gara LaMarche, "A Third Age Bill," *Democracy: A Journal of Ideas* (Spring 2008).

CHAPTER 8: THE GENERATIVITY REVOLUTION

164   *Phillip Longman, author of* The Empty Cradle: Phillip Longman, *The Empty Cradle: How Falling Birthrates Threaten World Prosperity and What to Do About It* (New York: Basic Books, 2004). See also Jonah Lehrer, "Fleeting Youth, Fading Creativity," *Wall Street Journal,* February 19, 2010.

164   *As* Newsweek *reported:* Stefan Theil, "The Golden Age of Innovation," *Newsweek,* August 20, 2010, http://www.newsweek.com/ 2010/08/20/innovation-grows-among-older-workers.html.

164   For research on David Galenson's work, see the following: David W. Galenson, *Old Masters and Young Geniuses: The Two Life Cycles of Artistic Creativity* (Princeton: Princeton University Press, 2006) and "World Shouldn't Look Past 'the Wisdom of the Elders,'" *USA Today,* November 7, 2007.

165   *Malcolm Gladwell:* Malcolm Gladwell, *What the Dog Saw, and Other Adventures* (New York: Little, Brown, 2009) as well as "Age Before Beauty," a February 21, 2006, speech at Columbia University.

166   *In the words of Mihaly Csikszentmihalyi:* Mihaly Csikszentmihalyi, Kevin Rathunde, and Samuel Whalen, *Talented Teenagers* (New York: Cambridge University Press, 1993).

168   *Apparently not to be outdone:* Phillip Longman, "Global Aging," *Foreign Policy,* November 2010.

168   *Galbraith—a boomer himself:* James K. Galbraith, "Why We Don't Need to Pay Down the National Debt," Atlantic.com, September 21, 2010.

169   *subtitle of the 2010 book* Shock of Gray: Ted C. Fishman, *Shock of Gray: The Aging of the World's Population and How It Pits Young Against Old, Child Against Parent, Worker Against Boss, Company*

Against Rival, and Nation Against Nation (New York: Scribner, 2010).

172 *Bill Clinton made this observation:* Eamon Javers, "Bill Clinton: New Talent Needed," *Politico*, April 29, 2010. See also Michael Vasquez, "Bill Clinton Delivers MDC Commencement Speech," *Miami Herald*, May 1, 2010; and Alex Katz, "Bill Clinton Brings Star Power to Lynch Party," *Boston Globe*, July 30, 2010.

173 *we face a new kind of deficit:* Andrew L. Yarrow and Marc Freedman, "Our 'Posterity Deficit': Americans Must Do More to Look Out for Future Generations," *Baltimore Sun*, January 12, 2010.

173 *Leon Kass, an ethics scholar:* Leon R. Kass, "L'Chaim and Its Limits: Why Not Immortality?" in *The Fountain of Youth: Cultural, Scientific, and Ethical Perspectives on a Biomedical Goal*, eds. Stephen G. Post and Robert H. Binstock (New York: Oxford University Press, 2004).

173 *As Harvard Medical School scholar:* George Vaillant, *Aging Well: Surprising Guideposts to a Happier Life from the Landmark Harvard Study of Adult Development* (Boston: Little, Brown, 2002).

174 *One poll by AARP found:* John M. Bridgeland, Robert D. Putnam, and Harris L. Wofford, *More to Give: Tapping the Talents of the Baby Boomer, Silent, and Greatest Generations* (Washington, DC: AARP, 2008), http://www.civicenterprises.net/pdfs/aarp_moreto-give.pdf.

174 *Another poll shows that boomers in particular:* John Zogby, "The Way We'll Be: The Baby Boomers' Legacy," Forbes.com, July 23, 2009.

174 *One* Wall Street Journal *headline from 2009:* Douglas Belkin, "Boomers to This Year's Grads: We Are Really, Really Sorry," *Wall Street Journal*, June 10, 2009.

RECOMMENDED READING LIST

Achenbaum, W. Andrew. "What Is Retirement For?" *Wilson Quarterly* (Spring 2006).

Andersen, Kurt. *Reset: How This Crisis Can Restore Our Values and Renew America*. New York: Random House, 2009.

Bateson, Mary Catherine. *Composing a Further Life: The Age of Active Wisdom*. New York: Alfred A. Knopf, 2010.

———. *Willing to Learn: Passages of Personal Discovery*. Hanover, NH: Steer Forth Press, 2004.

Bedell, Geraldine, and Rowena Young, eds. *The New Old Age: Perspectives on Innovating Our Way to the Good Life for All*. London: National Endowment for Science, Technology, and the Arts, 2009. http://www.nesta.org.uk/library/documents/the-new-old-age.pdf.

Bornstein, David. *How to Change the World: Social Entrepreneurs and the Power of New Ideas*. Updated ed. Oxford: Oxford University Press, 2007.

Bridges, William. *Transitions: Making Sense of Life's Changes*. New York: Perseus Books, 1980.

Buckley, Christopher. *Boomsday*. New York: Twelve, 2007.

Butler, Robert N. *The Longevity Revolution: The Benefits and Challenges of Living a Long Life*. New York: PublicAffairs, 2008.

Carstensen, Laura. *A Long Bright Future: An Action Plan for a Lifetime of Happiness, Health, and Financial Security*. New York: Broadway Books, 2009.

———. "On the Brink of a Brand-New Old Age." *New York Times*, January 2, 2001.

Cohen, Gene. *The Mature Mind: The Positive Power of the Aging Brain.* New York: Basic Books, 2007.

Cole, Thomas R. "The Prophecy of Senescence: G. Stanley Hall and the Reconstruction of Old Age in America." *Gerontologist* 24, no. 4 (1984): 360–366.

De St. Aubin, Ed, Dan P. McAdams, and Tae-Chang Kim, eds. *The Generative Society: Caring for Future Generations.* Washington, DC: American Psychological Association, 2003.

Dychtwald, Ken. *Age Power: How the 21st Century Will Be Ruled by the New Old.* New York: Penguin Putnam, 1999.

Dychtwald, Ken, and Daniel J. Kadlec. *With Purpose: Going from Success to Significance in Work and Life.* New York: Collins Living, 2009.

Englert, Jonathan. *The Collar.* New York: Houghton Mifflin, 2006.

Erikson, Erik H. *Identity: Youth and Crisis.* New York: W. W. Norton, 1968.

Erikson, Erik H., Joan M. Erikson, and Helen Q. Kivnick. *Vital Involvement in Old Age.* New York: W. W. Norton, 1994.

Farrell, Chris. *The New Frugality: How to Consume Less, Save More, and Live Better.* New York: Bloomsbury Press, 2009.

Friedan, Betty. *The Feminine Mystique.* New York: W. W. Norton, 1963.

———. *The Fountain of Age.* New York: Touchstone, 1993.

Fryer, Bronwyn. "Coping with 'Career Menopause.'" *Harvard Business Review* (blog), October 28, 2009. http://blogs.hbr.org/hbr/hbreditors/2009/10/coping_with_career_menopause.html.

Galenson, David W. *Old Masters and Young Geniuses: The Two Life Cycles of Artistic Creativity.* Princeton: Princeton University Press, 2006.

Gardner, John. *Self-Renewal: The Individual and the Innovative Society.* New York: W. W. Norton, 1995.

Hall, G. Stanley. *Senescence: The Last Half of Life.* New York: D. Appleton, 1922.

Hall, Stephen S. *Wisdom: From Philosophy to Neuroscience.* New York: Alfred A. Knopf, 2010.

Handy, Charles. *The Age of Unreason.* Boston: Harvard Business School Press, 1989.

———. *The Hungry Spirit.* New York: Broadway Books, 1998.

Hannon, Kerry. *What's Next? Follow Your Passion and Find Your Dream Job.* San Francisco: Chronicle Books, 2010.

Hareven, Tamara K. "The Last Stage: Historical Adulthood and Old Age." *Daedalus* 105, no. 4 (1976): 13–27.

"The HBR List: Breakthrough Ideas for 2005." *Harvard Business Review*, February 2005.

Hine, Thomas. *The Rise and Fall of the American Teenager*. New York: Harper Perennial, 2000.

Ibarra, Herminia. *Working Identity: Unconventional Strategies for Reinventing Your Career*. Boston: Harvard Business School Press, 2004.

"Interview with Carlo Strenger." *Learning to Lead Interview*, February 2009.

Kanter, Rosabeth Moss, Rakesh Khurana, and Nitin Nohria. "Moving Higher Education to Its Next Stage: A New Set of Societal Challenges, a New Stage of Life, and a Call to Action for Universities." Working paper, Harvard Business School, 2005.

Kass, Leon R. "L'Chaim and Its Limits: Why Not Immortality?" In *The Fountain of Youth: Cultural, Scientific, and Ethical Perspectives on a Biomedical Goal*, ed. Stephen G. Post and Robert H. Binstock. New York: Oxford University Press, 2004.

Kim, W. Chan, and Renée Mauborgne. *Blue Ocean Strategy: How to Create Uncontested Market Space and Make Competition Irrelevant*. Boston: Harvard Business School Press, 2005.

Kotre, John. *Outliving the Self: Generativity and the Interpretation of Lives*. Baltimore: Johns Hopkins University Press, 1984.

LaMarche, Gara. "A Third Age Bill." *Democracy: A Journal of Ideas*, no. 8 (Spring 2008).

Laslett, Peter. *A Fresh Map of Life: The Emergence of the Third Age*. Cambridge: Harvard University Press, 1991.

Lawrence-Lightfoot, Sara. *The Third Chapter: Passion, Risk, and Adventure in the 25 Years After 50*. New York: Farrar, Straus, and Giroux, 2009.

Levine, Suzanne Braun. *Fifty Is the New Fifty: Ten Life Lessons for Women in Second Adulthood*. New York: Viking Penguin, 2009.

———. *Inventing the Rest of Our Lives: Women in Second Adulthood*. New York: Viking Penguin, 2005.

Maestas, Nicole. "Back to Work: Expectations and Realizations of Work After Retirement." *Journal of Human Resources* 45, no. 3 (2010): 718–748.

McAdams, Dan P. *The Redemptive Self: Stories Americans Live By*. Oxford: Oxford University Press, 2005.

Miller, Mark. *The Hard Times Guide to Retirement Security: Practical Strategies for Money, Work, and Living*. Hoboken, NJ: Wiley, 2010.

Miller, Matt. *The Tyranny of Dead Ideas: Letting Go of the Old Ways of Thinking to Unleash a New Prosperity*. New York: Times Books, 2009.

Moen, Phyllis, and Patricia Roehling. *The Career Mystique: Cracks in the American Dream*. Lanham, MD: Rowman & Littlefield, 2005.

Morrow-Howell, Nancy, James Hinterlong, and Michael Sherraden. *Productive Aging*. Baltimore: Johns Hopkins University Press, 2006.

Moulden, Julia. *We Are the New Radicals: A Manifesto for Reinventing Yourself and Saving the World*. New York: McGraw-Hill, 2008.

Palladino, Grace. *Teenagers: An American History*. New York: Basic Books, 1996.

Parry, Manon. "G. Stanley Hall: Psychologist and Early Gerontologist." *American Journal of Public Health* 96, no. 7 (2006): 1160–1162.

Pink, Daniel H. *Drive: The Surprising Truth About What Motivates Us*. New York: Riverhead Books, 2009.

Ross, Dorothy. *G. Stanley Hall: The Psychologist as Prophet*. Chicago: University of Chicago Press, 1972.

———. "Granville Stanley Hall." In vol. 9 of *American National Biography*. New York: Oxford University Press, 1999.

Roszak, Theodore. *America the Wise: The Longevity Revolution and the True Wealth of Nations*. Boston: Houghton Mifflin, 1998.

Savage, Jon. *Teenage: The Prehistory of Youth Culture, 1875–1945*. New York: Penguin, 2008.

Shellenbarger, Sue. *The Breaking Point: How Today's Women Are Navigating the Midlife Crisis*. New York: Henry Holt, 2005.

Snarey, John. *How Fathers Care for the Next Generation: A Four-Decade Study*. Cambridge: Harvard University Press, 1993.

Steinem, Gloria. *Doing Sixty & Seventy*. San Francisco: Elders Academy Press, 2006.

Strauch, Barbara. *The Secret Life of the Grown-Up Brain: The Surprising Talents of the Middle-Aged Mind*. New York: Viking, 2010.

Strenger, Carlo, and Arie Ruttenberg. "The Existential Necessity of Midlife Change." *Harvard Business Review*, February 2008.

Vaillant, George E. *Adaptation to Life*. Boston: Little, Brown, 1977.

———. *Aging Well: Surprising Guideposts to a Happier Life from the Landmark Harvard Study of Adult Development*. Boston: Little, Brown, 2002.

Whitbourne, Susan Krauss. *The Search for Fulfillment: Revolutionary New Research That Reveals the Secret to Long-Term Happiness.* New York: Ballantine Books, 2010.

Woodward, Kathleen. "Against Wisdom: The Social Politics of Anger and Aging." *Journal of Aging Studies* 17 (2003): 55–67.

THE BIG SHIFT
DISCUSSION GUIDE
Getting the Conversation Started

It's time to make a big shift—from reading to talking.

The Big Shift should be an easy conversation starter among your friends, neighbors, and colleagues. After all, one of the major points of the book is that, despite feelings to the contrary, we're not alone in this new stage of life. There are millions of us.

Here are twenty questions to help launch discussions at work, the library, your place of worship, your book group, or your local senior center.

1. Marc Freedman opens the book with a story about reserving a hotel room with two cribs using his AARP discount card. Have you experienced similar disconnects or seeming contradictions in your own life?
2. Do you agree with Freedman that there's a new life stage between midlife and old age with a unique set of characteristics and needs? If yes, what are your experiences in this new stage?
3. There are two new stages of life making news. Do you see parallels between the idea of extended adolescence ("emerging adulthood") and this new stage ("mature adulthood")?
4. Freedman writes about his health scare—a tremor that threatened Parkinson's disease. Is an increased sense of mortality, or a sense

of how much healthy time you may have left, a factor for you? How does it affect decisions about how you plan your life?

5. What's your take on the personal midlife crisis—real or imagined? What versions of it have you witnessed? Have you experienced one of your own?

6. Do you think there is a societal midlife crisis affecting millions today and future generations tomorrow? What are the consequences—and what can be done?

7. Before reading this book, did you think about longer lives as a problem or an opportunity—or both? Did Freedman change your mind?

8. Do you feel like you're navigating this new stage of life alone? Are you proceeding in a DIY way? What kind of help do you wish you had?

9. Have you turned to any institutions or organizations for help, connection, and education or retraining as you think about and plan your postmidlife years? Was it useful? Why or why not?

10. Would you consider investing time and resources in developing new skills? Would you, for example, borrow money to go back to school?

11. In Chapter 2, Meredith McKenzie radically alters her lifestyle so she can work for an environmental nonprofit. Would you consider doing the same? Is working for a nonprofit salary an option for you? What lifestyle changes are you willing to make?

12. Given fifty-year working lives, instead of the thirty-year working lives more common in the past, how should people plan their educations and finance their futures? Should government play a role?

13. Do you think about working longer as a burden or as a chance to do the things you've always wanted to do?

14. Do you feel the impulse to give back that Freedman describes as generativity? Do you feel it more as you get older?

15. When you consider the prospect of living longer, it's most appealing if the years are added to the middle of your life, not the

end. What do you think are the best ways for millions of people to make sure that they extend midlife instead of old age?

16. Are you surprised that so many people over fifty are starting businesses and nonprofit organizations? Is that something you've considered? What attracts you to the idea—or discourages you from trying it?

17. In Chapter 7 Freedman lists ten changes he'd like to see. What would you add to his list?

18. Do you think this new stage of life presents an opportunity for personal and societal change as dramatic as the opportunities presented by the women's movement and the civil rights movement?

19. Have you been inspired by anyone in the book—or any idea in the book—to make a change in your thinking or your life? By whom or by what?

20. If one hundred–year life spans become the norm, what changes do you foresee at all stages of life?

If you would like to spread the word about *The Big Shift*, or host a book group discussion, please go to http://www.encore.org/thebigshift.

INDEX

ABOUT THE AUTHOR

by Liz Lynch

Marc Freedman is CEO and founder of Civic Ventures. He spearheaded the creation of Experience Corps, now one of America's largest nonprofit national service programs engaging people over fifty-five, and the Purpose Prize, which annually provides five $100,000 prizes to social innovators in the second half of life.

Freedman is the author of *Encore: Finding Work That Matters in the Second Half of Life*, *Prime Time: How Baby Boomers Will Revolutionize Retirement and Transform America*, and *The Kindness of Strangers: Adult Mentors, Urban Youth, and the New Voluntarism*.

Recognized by *Fast Company* magazine in 2007, 2008, and 2009 as one of the nation's leading social entrepreneurs, Freedman is widely published and quoted in the national media and has been honored with numerous awards and fellowships, including an Ashoka Senior Fellowship, the Maxwell A. Pollack Award of the Gerontological Society of America, the Archstone Award of the American Public Health Association, and membership in the Innovators Network of the Japan Society. The *NonProfit Times* named him one of the fifty most powerful and influential individuals in the nonprofit sector in 2010. Freedman and Civic Ventures received the 2010 Skoll Award for Social Entrepreneurship at Oxford University in April of that year.

A high honors graduate of Swarthmore College, Freedman has an MBA from Yale University and was a Visiting Research Fellow of Kings College, University of London. He lives with his wife and children in the San Francisco Bay Area. For more information, go to: www.encore.org/thebigshift or www.bigshift.org.

PublicAffairs is a publishing house founded in 1997. It is a tribute to the standards, values, and flair of three persons who have served as mentors to countless reporters, writers, editors, and book people of all kinds, including me.

I. F. STONE, proprietor of *I. F. Stone's Weekly*, combined a commitment to the First Amendment with entrepreneurial zeal and reporting skill and became one of the great independent journalists in American history. At the age of eighty, Izzy published *The Trial of Socrates*, which was a national bestseller. He wrote the book after he taught himself ancient Greek.

BENJAMIN C. BRADLEE was for nearly thirty years the charismatic editorial leader of *The Washington Post*. It was Ben who gave the *Post* the range and courage to pursue such historic issues as Watergate. He supported his reporters with a tenacity that made them fearless and it is no accident that so many became authors of influential, best-selling books.

ROBERT L. BERNSTEIN, the chief executive of Random House for more than a quarter century, guided one of the nation's premier publishing houses. Bob was personally responsible for many books of political dissent and argument that challenged tyranny around the globe. He is also the founder and longtime chair of Human Rights Watch, one of the most respected human rights organizations in the world.

·   ·   ·

For fifty years, the banner of Public Affairs Press was carried by its owner Morris B. Schnapper, who published Gandhi, Nasser, Toynbee, Truman, and about 1,500 other authors. In 1983, Schnapper was described by *The Washington Post* as "a redoubtable gadfly." His legacy will endure in the books to come.

Peter Osnos, *Founder and Editor-at-Large*